You!! The Next Millionaire

You!! The Next Millionaire

Jaya Raj Kozandapani
with
Nickleirsch & Sharinni

PARTRIDGE
A Penguin Random House Company

To order additional copies of this book, contact
Toll Free 800 101 2657 (Singapore)
Toll Free 1 800 81 7340 (Malaysia)
orders.singapore@partridgepublishing.com

www.partridgepublishing.com/singapore

Contents and Titles   Page/s

DEDICATION AND GRATITUDE

This work is a product of inspiration by hundreds of people whom I have analysed in my entire life. Due to God given ability, I was able to dissect every bit of people's character, habit, attitude and mindset which ultimately form the type of dream these people often choose to dream that eventually leads to the type of life they live. My Thanks to all!

I would however choose to specifically highlight the names of these people below for being great support to me in the works I do. I feel a deep sense of gratitude:

-wife Mala and my two kids for their kindness and understanding while I incessantly work day and night.

-to my mom for the love and whom I owe all.

-to friends Thiagarajan Marimuthu, Dato' Muthu (JB), Justin R, Yap (Singapore), Joe (KL), S.Brian Ravi, Victor Rajavel, Atchuthan, K. Murali, Anthony Rajan, VGR Chandran, Ponnusamy, B.Saravanan, Vasaga M (Terry), Jeevanand, S. Jeyamani, Puthiran, Ramesh Murugan and Ronald Mak for being great mentors, motivators and above all greatest inspirations...

-to my bosses at Stadpharm Pharmaceuticals, Jimmy Khoo and Marina Choo for their patience and encouragements..

-to my one and only brother L.Jayabalan for his constant love and interest.

Jaya Raj Kozandapani with Nickleirsch & Sharinni

-to my loyal customers Dr Suthakar, Dr Nidyananda and Dr Adrian Seah for their continued support and trust.

-to the happy memory of my father, grandpa and grandma.. (will always love y'all)

SEARCHING FOR WEALTH

95% of us, think that the way to get our hands to wealth is a well-guarded secret reserved for the chosen 5% of the population. This is not a rule, neither man-made or natural. It is not a rule but just mere true statistics. We all know that 90% of the wealth of the world are in the hands of 5% population of the world. The one mistake we make is looking outside of us for the things that can be manifested inside of us. This holds true for all things in life. Money is no exception. Now let me explain this through an example. Just imagine the people that lived in the past. Many hundred or even many thousand years ago. They did not have all the things surrounding us that we now take for granted as necessity. Tap water for instance. Imagine a world where there is no tap water facility. A village that you need to wake up early to fetch water from the well and everyone else is also doing the same. Will that condition deprive you of happiness? Certainly NO! Just as the source of true happiness lies within each of us, so is the source of wealth! Money is the result of a very specific mental attitude. Call it what you like: the mentality of the rich, of millionaires, or of successful men. Money is the outward manifestation of an inner focus, of thoughts being steered towards a specific target. Unfortunately, most people are unaware of this. The major principles we will examine in the following chapter all lead to a higher, universal truth – that the mind is capable of anything. Genuine wealth is, above all, a state of mind – a state that has taken form in the lives of the rich. We must begin by being rich in mind before we can become rich in life.

Wealth is derived by altering the state of the mind

Gaining a clear understanding of the subconscious is fundamental. It is all very well to tell people that they must believe in success and fortune, and want it passionately. Yet, most people are paralysed by bad experiences. In addition, they appear totally incapable of cultivating what Nietzsche called "the will to power". It is not all easy to demand action and firmness from someone who is irresolute, passive, and unmotivated. By discovering the mechanisms and power of the subconscious mind, however, anyone can overcome this obstacle. So, let us examine the subconscious mind, the source of man's greatest personal and material wealth – the one and only place to look for the money that grows on trees. Soon you will learn how to tap into it at will.

THE INFINITE POSSIBILITIES WITHIN YOU

IT'S ALL IN THE ATTITUDE

You and only you is capable of creating your own happiness or misery, a fact that cannot be denied by anyone who has mastered the laws of the mind, even superficially. This maxim probably isn't new to you. Some of you may have greeted it with skepticism, while some of you may believe in it wholeheartedly. Nevertheless, there aren't many people who have thought it over carefully or measured the full extent of its consequences. This is where the game is.

The lives of the rich men we examine reveal that each one of them made full use of his subconscious mind to become wealthy. The key to success ultimately lies in the proper use of the subconscious mind. "Why?" you might ask. The reason is that both the means to make money and the outside circumstances affecting us are so varied and personal that it would be impossible to propose a surefire winning formula. Besides, no miracle recipe exists. It would be too simple. What does exists, however, and thousands of brilliant success stories testify to this, is a positive inner attitude.

Many books deal with the secrets of real estate, the stock market, management, and so forth. These books are obviously invaluable reference tools. But the advice they ladle out, no matter how precise it is, is inevitably, always general. Pretending otherwise would be naïve and dishonest. In fact, however instructive a book claims to be, it will not tell you whether you should accept a job that comes your way, bid on a house, or invest in a particular money

11

making proposition. Each case is unique. Even if your preliminary studies are very comprehensive, there are always imponderables in any scheme. Any analysis will be inadequate. We're not saying that it's unnecessary. On the contrary, improvisation and rashness are usually inadvisable. What we do mean is that there are times that your analysis can go no further. This is when a person's sixth sense, what some people also call "business sense", "luck", or "intuition", comes into play – the result of positive mental programming and a well-utilized subconscious mind. This is what makes the difference between a successful and an unsuccessful person. This is the essence which will open the doors. This is the platform where you stand strong and the universe start sourcing the wealth you need. When you succeeded in your mental programming; your thought waves are going to permeate to every nooks and corners of the universe demanding attention from the entire cosmos. The universe then have no choice but to offer itself to your intentions and desire.

WHAT IS THE SUBCONSCIOUS?

We have all at some time or other heard talks about the subconscious mind. Its existence is now accepted in all scientific fields, although its final definition is still a matter of dispute. We have no intention of engaging in a long theoretical or historical analysis here. Let us simply state, without getting bogged down by theoretical details, that the human mind can be divided into two parts: the conscious and the subconscious. The most common image used to illustrate the importance of the two parts is an iceberg, the small visible part being considered the conscious mind, the submerged and much larger part, the subconscious. This analogy was commonly used by Sigmund Freud (the father of Psychology) to explain the above to his students.

In fact, the role the subconscious has to play in our lives is much greater than we believe it to be. It is the seat of our habits, complexes, and the limitations of our personalities. No matter what we think, the subconscious – not outside circumstances – is responsible for an individual's wealth or poverty.

The subconscious can be compared to a computer. It blindly and infallibly executes the programme fed into it. Every individual is programmed whether he knows it or not, and most people are programmed negatively. Given that the subconscious is phenomenally powerful, a person who has been programmed in this way will unfortunately never be successful or wealthy.

HOW IS THE SUBCONSCIOUS PROGRAMMED?

As long as individual remains unaware of the laws of the mind, he will stay ignorant of his own programming. This is the case with most people, for a very simple reason. Mental programming takes place very early in a person's childhood, at an age when his critical sense is still undeveloped. He naturally accepts all suggestions from the outside world. These suggestions, the program's data base, so to speak, come at first from his parents and teachers. They become engraved in his young mind, which is as impressionable as a piece of soft wax. A single word can often blight someone's life or at least weigh him down for a long time to come. This word may have been said without malice, but its effects can be disastrous. As for examples, there are plenty to choose from. A pessimistic mother, oppressed by misery, will tell a child she considers too impulsive or absent-minded, 'You'll never get rich.' Or, 'You'll never get anywhere in life,' or, "You'll be a loser, just like your father." These remarks are recorded in the child's subconscious, becoming part of his mental programming. The subconscious, whose power is almost limitless, will do its utmost to execute this programme, making the child fail over and over again. The most tragic thing of all is that this person can spend his entire life unaware that he is the victim of negative mental programming.

HOW A FEW WORDS CAN CHANGE YOUR LIFE

You might be skeptical about the effects of an apparently insignificant word or phrase, but words are extremely powerful agents. A declaration of love, a piece of bad news, a word of congratulation, all have an impact on our inner state. And what is most astonishing is that these words, which are actually suggestions, as we shall see further on in this chapter, do not even have to be true for the mind to accept them. Let's say your boss congratulates you on the job you have done. Perhaps he is not really all that satisfied with it, but since he knows that you are having marital difficulties, getting divorced, say, he judges its best not to reproach you. His words of encouragement, although insincere, raise your low morale and revitalize you. This is only one example among many of the power words can have.

The authors of that remarkable book, *In Search of Excellence*, recount an experiment that illustrates the principle of the power of words even when those words are untrue.

The old adage is "nothing succeeds like success". It turns out to have a sound scientific basis. Researchers studying motivation find that the prime factor is simply the self-perception among motivated subjects that they are, in fact, doing well. Whether they are or not by any absolute standard doesn't seem to matter much. In one experiment, adults were given 10 puzzles to solve. All 10 were exactly the same for all subjects. They worked on them, turned them in, and were given the results at the end. Now, in fact, the results they were given were fictitious. Half of the exam takers were told that they had done well, with seven out of 10 correct. The other half were told they had done poorly, with seven out of 10 wrong. Than all were given another 10 puzzles (the same for each person). The half who had been *told* that they had done well in the first round really did do better in the second, and the other half really did do worse. Mere association with past personal success apparently leads to more persistence, higher motivation, or something that makes us do better. Warren Bennis, in *The Unconscious Conspiracy: Why leaders can't lead,* finds ample reason to agree: "In a study of school teachers, it turned out that when they held high expectations of their students, that alone was enough to cause an increase of 25 points in the students' IQ scores."

The results of these experiments are food for thought. The subjects' subconscious minds had been influenced by the falsified results. It is this and this alone which radically improved one group's performance and weakened the other's.

A little further on, the same authors advance the following theory as a result of this experiment: "We often argue that the excellent companies are the way they are because they are organized to obtain extraordinary effort from ordinary human beings. " What applies to business applies equally to individuals. This is why it is so astonishing that seemingly unexceptional people achieve such extraordinary results. Their secret: a well-guided subconscious mind.

Each individual is programmed. Parents, teachers, and friends are programming agents who are often clumsy and harmful, using negative words without realizing the impact they have. There is also another very important programming agent: the individual himself. All of us have our own inner monologues. We repeat to ourselves: "Things aren't going very well, are they?" "I'm always tired," "Why am I not succeeding?" "I'm overworked," "I'll never find a job," "I'll never get a raise," " I'll never be rich," or " I'm not talented enough." These negative, pessimistic thoughts that you more or less consciously repeat to yourself are all suggestions that influence your subconscious or reinforce its current programme. Needless to say, these thoughts must definitely be driven out of your mind. Let's see how.

IT'S NEVER TOO LATE TO GROW RICH

It is reassuring that proof exists showing that no programme is irreversible. Just as we can modify or revamp a computer programme, we can completely overhaul our personalities, which are moulded in the subconscious mind. Experiments carried out on many subjects have demonstrated that it generally takes thirty days to set up a new programme.

How can we acquire a personality that will magically attract success and trigger favourable circumstances? See here that we not only attract success but TRIGGER FAVOURABLE CIRCUMSTANCES. We can rely on a wide variety of methods currently available, which are based on self-suggestion. These methods often carry different names. Some authors speak of the Alpha method, others of psycho-cybernetics, mental programming, positive thinking, or self-hypnosis. All of these techniques are basically valid, yet, each is a variation or adaptation of an astonishingly simple method developed by a French pharmacist, Emile Coue'. His discovery was accidental. One day, one of his clients insisted on buying a drug for which he needed a prescription. Faced with this client's stubbornness, Emile Coue' thought up a trick. He recommended a product to him that was ostensibly just as effective, but which was actually a sugar-pill. The patient came back a few days later, completely cured and absolutely delighted with the results. What was later to be called the placebo effect had just been discovered!

What had happened to this patient? Well, it was basically the same phenomenon that had occurred in the experiment in In *Search of Excellence,* except that the magical effect of words, of confidence and of the subconscious had acted on the physical, rather than intellectual level. This subject was cured by his confidence in the pharmacist and in the medication, as well as by the mental certainty that he was going to get well.

It didn't take Emile Coue' long to realize the significance of this experiment. If a word could cure an ailment, what could it do to someone's personality? In the next few years he developed an extremely simply formula which has been applied throughout the world and has improved the lives of thousands of individuals. Why self-suggestion? Since Coue' couldn't stay at each patient's bedside, or stay in contact with him, the patient could cure himself using his own chosen formula.

Here is the formula Coue' developed:

Every day, and in every way I am getting better and better

He advises people to repeat this formula aloud in a monotone voice about 20 times a day. Countless variations have been developed. You will soon be able to concoct your own according to your needs and personality. The effects it produces are astounding. This general formula embraces all aspects of existence and has infinite possibilities. It must be repeated on a daily basis. Repetition is the golden rule of self-suggestion. We must literally flood our subconscious with this saying. A new programme will set in little by little, and a new personality along with it. Negative reinforcement will give way to positive reinforcement, enthusiasm, energy, boldness, and determination. Don't get put off by the apparent simplicity of this method like several of Emile Coue's contemporaries, who refused to believe that such a simple technique could be effective. Remember, your negative programming is intent on survival. Practising this method threatens its existence and will overcome any scepticism.

Every day, and in every way. I am getting better and better

The rich men biographies, whose lives we delved into did not always use these formulas explicitly. And yet, faced with adversity, each of them subconsciously resorted to them. The principles outlined in many rich people's biographies are proof of this. We encourage you to read the biographies of your role models, as many as you want and you will realize the above is true indeed. Whether confronted by problems or on the threshold of a new adventure, each of them had learned to condition or programme himself by repeating that he was going to be successful, that no obstacle would short-circuit his attempts.

Many rich and famous personalities have revealed in their autobiographies that a large part of success was due to a personalized variation of self-suggestion. We leave it to you to analyse your own role models because your circumstances, your talent and your capacity only you know best. You must not compare yourself only to the top 10 richest people in the world per se. You can take a look at your well to do uncle, friend or anyone you like in your own country.

Here's an example of an autobiography of a very rich and relevant personality :

I learned how to keep problems from crushing me. I refused to worry about more than one thing at a time, and I would not let useless fretting about a problem, no matter how important, keep me from sleeping. This is easier said than done. I may have read a book on the subject, I don't remember, but in any case I worked out a system that allowed me to turn off nervous tension and shut out nagging questions when I went to bed. I knew if I didn't, I wouldn't be bright and fresh and be able to deal with customers in the morning. I would think of my mind as being a blackboard full of messages, most of them urgent, and I practiced imagining a hand with an eraser wiping that blackboard clean. I made my mind completely blank. If a thought began to appear, zap! I'd wipe it out before it could form. Then I would relax my body, beginning at the back of my neck and continuing on down: shoulders, arms, torso, legs, to the tips of my toes. By this time I would be asleep. I learned to do this procedure rather rapidly. Others marveled that I could work 12 or 14 hours a day at a busy convention, then entertain potential customers until two or three o'clock in the morning, and still be out of bed early, ready to collar my next client. My secret was in getting the most out of every moment of rest. I guess I couldn't have averaged more than six hours of sleep a night. Many times I got four hours or less. But I slept as hard as I worked.

The above person's technique is preceded by physical relaxation. Physical and mental relaxation go hand in hand. Furthermore, in a state of relaxation our brain waves slow down and the subconscious is much more open to suggestion.

There is obviously a broad range of relaxation techniques available on the market. If you already know one, so much the better. If not, here is a very simple one.

HOW TO RELAX

Lie down on the floor or in bed, or seat yourself comfortably in an armchair. Close your eyes. Inhale deeply about 10 times. Then relax each separate part of your body, beginning with your feet and going up towards your head. This technique, by the way, is popularly called "autogenic training".

Once you are feeling very relaxed, start repeating your suggestion. Emile Coue's well-known formula is excellent for obtaining results in every aspect of your life. But you can also work on more specific elements. In order to apply the principles we will be discussing, you will have to develop certain qualities. In fact, with this method of self-suggestion, you can transform your personality and become the person you have always dreamed o being. Make an outline of the qualities you would like to have or perfect. To help you do this, here is a list of the basic characteristics shared by most of the rich and famous. Millionaires are usually:

• Tenacious	Confident
• Enthusiastic	Imaginative
• Energetic	Diligent
• Bold	Positive
• Intuitive	Astute
• Persuasive	Dependable
• Authoritative	Daring

Choose the qualities you lack or need to work on the most. Work on one at a time, starting with your weakest point. You will see how much stronger you will be just by eliminating one of them.

A simple way of making up your own formula is by varying Emile Coue's famous one. You could select one of the qualities listed above and say to yourself, "Every day, and in every way, I am becoming more and more enthusiastic," or "Every day, and in every way, I am becoming more and more energetic." Create your own suggestions. Choose simple words that are the most familiar and evocative to you. Write your suggestions down on paper. The simple act of writing a suggestion down will have a great impact on you, giving your thoughts more power and authority. It becomes a concrete action. It is the springboard for the action you will take, the starting point of your personality change. Never lose sight of your suggestions. Re-read them often. They will soon be part of your life. The old person within you will be replaced by a younger one who will fulfill your aims and guide your actions. Here are a few other basic rules for making up your own suggestions. Experience has shown that, to be fully effective, suggestions must be:

Brief If they are too long they will not be effective.

Positive This is absolutely essential. The subconscious works differently from the conscious mind. If you say, "I'm not poor anymore," the word *poor* might be retained since it is the key word. It could have the opposite result. Say this instead: "I'm becoming rich."

Gradual Some authors state that we must formulate our suggestions as if we already had what we desired. This could be counter-productive, however. Our conscious mind sees a contradiction here. Mental conflict may arise which might compromise the positive results of the suggestion. So, if you repeat "I'm rich," or "My job is perfect," your mind will naturally sense the inconsistency here, especially if you are broke or out of work. It would be better to say, "I'm getting richer day by day," or "I'm getting a perfect job."

These formulas will guarantee you success. One way of avoiding conflict is by repeating key words without any verbs. One of the most powerful words associations you could use is the following:

Success - wealth

Repeat these words over and over. This is the goal you are now aiming for.

Here is a powerful variation of Emile Coue's formula. It is a little longer, but if you like it, it will accomplish marvellous things for you.

"Every day, and in every way, things are getting better and better and I am growing richer in every area of my life"

Even a mechanical and barely convincing repetition of these words has some effect. However, the more emotion and feeling you put into your suggestion, the better the results will be. Remember emotions are energy. We need energy to fuel our intentions and desires. If you want something with every ounce of your body, mind, and soul, your dreams will be realized. Thomas Edison once said that years of experience had taught him that any man who wants something so badly that he will gamble his future on one roll of the dice is sure to win.

Wealthy men put all of their hearts into their endeavours and their desire to succeed was fuelled by unwavering passion. Be bold enough to imitate them. Don't be afraid to listen to your heart. Start programming yourself today. There is enough power to transform your life and make you wealthy in this chapter alone, yet no one can make you rich but yourself. No one can repeat these formulas for you. Your first step should therefore be to repeat the formulas you have chosen.

YOU'LL NEVER GET RICH IF YOU CAN'T PICTURE YOURSELF RICH

Everyone who wants to become rich must convince himself thoroughly of this. Similarly, anyone who sees himself as nothing but a slow employee and who cannot imagine ever being able to scale the corporate ladder will stay in this position for the rest of his life.

The result of all inner programming is called your "self-image" in psycho-cybernetic terms. Despite our conscious efforts to create a self-image, each of us has only a vague idea of the role self-image plays in our lives. It is important to understand this since people are what they believe themselves to be. Everything in your life, including your degree of wealth, is directly proportional to your self-image.

You must therefore give serious thought to the premise that the greatest limitation man can impose on himself is the one created in his own mind. Similarly, the greatest freedom he can enjoy is mental freedom.

How is your self-image created? Well, it follows the same process as your mental programming, since your self-image is a faithful reflection of it. In fact, it is the conscious part of your mental programming. As we stated previously, most individuals are unaware of the impact that self-image has on their lives. Their self-images are basically shaped by two primary sources: the external world, including parents, teachers, friends, and acquaintance, and the inner world, namely, the thoughts that they have.

Man's greatest limitation is the one created in his own mind.

Stop and analyse this principle for a minute or two. It could very well start you on the road to a totally new life. How do you picture yourself? Do you believe that you could easily double your income within a year? You don't? Rest assured, life will prove you right, since this belief has been programmed into your subconscious, whether you realize it or not. You have given your mind a command – a negative command. You have entered a limit into your subconscious and it will put everything into motion to run this programme as best it can. Your subconscious is very powerful and has a vast memory bank

at its disposal. The problems it will come across to prevent you from doubling your yearly income will be formidable. It is therefore just as hard for you to fail as to succeed. It is just as easy for you to succeed as it is to fail.

In the following chapter, we will discuss the importance of goals. Now that you are aware of the mechanisms of the subconscious, you know that an objective is simply a specific programme that you enter into your subconscious. By the way, do you know what you must base your goal on? The answer might surprise you. Despite certain outside factors that will inevitably come into play here, you will automatically establish your goal according to your self-image.

> Establish your goals according to your self-image

First of all you might say to yourself: "I want to increase my yearly income by £10,000." That's good. It's legitimate and absolutely possible. It will most likely enhance your lifestyle significantly, even if the Inland Revenue grabs a large chunk of it. But why did you limit yourself to £10,000? The reason is simple: the image you have of yourself is of a person who can only get £10,000 richer in a year. We don't mean to dismiss this goal in any way. We could have chosen £2,500 or £100,000. This figure is arbitrary, chosen merely for the purposes of demonstration, but you must ask yourself what is "reasonably" preventing you from increasing your income even more substantially? There isn't one valid constraint. Do you know how much Steven Spielberg earned in 1982 after ET had been released?

Over one million dollars a day! Now you can see that your goals are limited only by the mind.

Therefore, the starting point for growing rich and surpassing yourself is to expand your self-image, or better yet, remould it. A new self-image will produce a new goal, and a new goal will result in a new life for you. This appears simple, but it is constantly being confirmed.

All rich men pictured themselves rich
before achieving their dreams

No matter how poor they were at the beginning, no matter how little education they had, no matter how few contacts they enjoyed, all of them pictured themselves rich before making their fortunes. All of them were convinced that they would one day become millionaires. Life answered their dreams in accordance with their self-image and the faith that they had in their success.

To try to discover your self-image, tell yourself, for example: I'm going to be very rich," Now analyse your reactions. Remember, there is an exact ratio between your ego and what life offers you. You can change it at any time, however, according to your aspirations. In the beginning, when your begin reprogramming yourself and shaping a new self-image, you will see that you will inevitably be influenced by your old image. This is completely normal. Change takes place in gradual stages.

Create your own self-image. Nothing is easier. Rely on the method we exposed earlier on. Here are a few formulas that you can use. Later you will add your financial goal, setting a precise amount and a deadline for reaching it. We will explain how to do this further on.

- "I'm getting richer day by day."
- "I'm going to find an ideal job that will satisfy all my needs."

- "Life is putting the people who will help me improve my financial situation directly in my path."
- "I'm going to meet the ideal partner."
- "I'm going to find a way to double my yearly income."
- "All my abilities are getting better, allowing me to increase my income."
- "I'm going to keep going until I succeed."
- "It's easy for me to reach all my goals."
- "I'm going to find the situation that will help me perfect my qualities and talents."

When creating your own formulas (if those we have recommended don't suit you) don't impose limitations on yourself. Don't be afraid to be bold when setting your objectives. The potential you have is extraordinary. Develop it. People who become wealthy are not ostensibly any different from you. The mental limits they set for themselves are simply unlike your own. The amounts they earn in an hour might impress you. But do you think it impresses them? Generally not. Their earnings are the result of a highly ordinary, normal mental programme for them. It can be the same for you. Ray Kroc once said, "Think big and you'll become big."

RAY KROC

> I have always believed that every man creates his own happiness and is responsible for his own problems

REMOVE YOUR MENTAL BLOCK

Creating a new self-image inevitably entails making a clean sweep of the old one. Yet, everybody puts up fight, attempting to resist this change. One of the most common, deeply embedded and harmful mental blocks is the idea that 'money is dirty'. This notion manifests itself in different ways and is generally a subconscious one. People will tell you that it is unhealthy to want to get rich, and that those who wish to improve their lot in life are unscrupulous capitalists and vulgar materialists. These ideas are the vestiges of a puritanism. An aversion to money, however, is often hypocritical. People malign the rich, but secretly envy them. Now here's something important to remember. NEVER BE ONE OF THEM. This is one very bad mindset to get you far from attaining wealth, and if you're unluckier still, will make you remain stuck in poverty. It should nevertheless be noted that attitudes are gradually changing, even though certain prejudices remain.

Another common hang-up is fear of going against family background and upbringing. Not everyone suffers from this, of course. We have already seen that the frustration and humiliation bred by poverty have been catalysts for many fortunes, proving that humble origins do not condemn people to mediocrity and that poverty is not hereditary. No matter how shocking this may sound, poverty is in many cases a form of mental illness.

This is reassuring to some extent. If poverty is an illness, it can be cured. People can get out of it. There are no external conditions, constraints, or circumstances that the mind cannot overcome. Anyone who understands this truth can become successful and shape his present and future life to match his aspirations. Anyone who becomes aware of this fundamental law and applies it to his life can become whatever he wants to be. And nothing, absolutely nothing, can stop him. Circumstances will bend to his wishes. This is nothing new. You would have seen many miraculous turn of events in your life even before you read this book. That is because you already use your subconscious mind without realizing in the past. Now that you have seen it, go for " bigger, better, bolder ".

THE TRUE SIGNIFICANCE OF MONEY

The view that money is dirty and that people deny their origins by raising themselves above their family expectations is indeed a deplorable one. The idea that anyone who has monetary ambitions is a mean-spirited capitalist is completely misguided. Apart from the money people inherit or win by chance in lotteries or at the races, what does making a lot of money mean? Money which has been earned honestly is simply a recognition of services rendered. A rich man is therefore one who has provided services to many people and has been justly rewarded for them. This is what most of those who scorn money forget when they condemn it. Steve Job accumulated billions and billions of dollars. But what did he offer in exchange? Thanks to his patience, genius, and determination, this man, sometimes the laughing-stock of his peers, made mankind take a giant step forward. Can you imagine life nowadays without Apple? Of course not. Furthermore, he helped create thousands of jobs. He was attending meetings and conferences even till his last days, before succumbing to liver cancer. His fortune is a symbol of public recognition, the just payment for services rendered. Henry Ford was another example. He was the first to start the automobile business even though it is widely believed that he was not the only pioneer to invent the automobile. He was perfectly aware of the real value of money, and that awareness taught him the surest way of getting it. When a man asked him one day what he would do if he lost his entire fortune, he answered without batting an eyelid that he would think up another fundamental human need and meet it by offering a cheaper and more efficient service than anybody else. He went on to say that he would be a millionaire again within five years.

Finding a basic need and answering it with cheaper, more efficient service ; this is how most rich people build their fortunes. We could establish the same equation for 99% of millionaires and billionaires of the current world.

Think of Walt Disney. He brightened the lives of thousands of children. Thomas Watson? His business genius allowed him to market IBM computers and to change our society. What would modern life be like without computers? Conrad Hilton? His hotel policy guaranteed travellers all over the world exceptional quality and comfort, and this earned him his fortune.

Those who criticize these men for having too much money should consider what they did for their fellow man in terms of products, services and employment. The recognition these men received was well earned.

What counts is the quality of the product or service. A single idea can lead to affluence. Putting it into operation, however, obviously requires more time and effort.

Rubik, the creator of the mind-boggling Rubik Cube, became a millionaire with a single idea. Which service did he offer the public? He amused thousands of people all over the world by making them rack their brains. And how much do you think the inventor of "Monopoly" made in royalties?

Many people believe that money in itself is neither good nor bad. We, on the other hand, believe that money is the golden key of civilization. It is no coincidence that the richest countries in the world have also reached the highest cultural and scientific levels. The advantages of money are enormous, for individuals as well as for entire societies. So, get rid once and for all your medieval ideas that money is dirty, degrading, and evil. Naturally, we are not naïve enough to claim that money is a cure-all, but it does make life easier and it opens a lot of doors. The only danger is becoming a slave to it. Money is an excellent servant, but it is an autocratic master. What is most important is to integrate a positive view of money into your new self-image. It is your passport to greater freedom. You are entitled to it. Exercise this right. Get rid of whatever mental blocks you have about money. Until you do, you will never be able to grow rich. Be vigilant, however. This inhibition often comes disguised in insidious forms in order to escape your attention. While analyzing your ideas, keep in mind the following principle: **There is no valid reason why you cannot become rich.**

PICTURE YOURSELF RICH ALREADY!

A picture is worth a thousand words, or so the saying goes. We have seen how to use verbal suggestions to change your self-image and to reprogramme your subconscious mind. These suggestions suit many people perfectly and are always effective. However some people like to add guided imagery to them, Creative visualization can be a great help. We all use it every day in our lives. We think in images as much as in words. We constantly give in to what is popularly called "daydreaming' or "wakeful dreaming'.

We plan out our futures and evoke memories of the past, reliving them in images. Whether we know it or not, these images greatly influence our subconscious and help shape our personalities. In fact, they often mould our futures without our knowing it. If this is done in a positive way, there is nothing left to say. But since this imagery is generally not guided, it often has a negative effect on us. Constant memories of sadness or failure reinforce our negative programming. If we are pessimistic by nature, negative images permeate our dreams of the future, often fulfilling our expectations.

Mental imagery must therefore be steered in the right direction. Every day, make sure that the time you devote to reprogramming yourself is accompanied by creative visualization, or 'scientific dreaming' as some call it. Once you are relaxed, fill your mind with new and positive images. There is no limit to what you can do. Pretend that you already have what you are hoping for, and that your goal has already been reached. One of the reasons why this technique is so effective is that the subconscious is not governed by the same temporal rules as the conscious mind. In fact, time does not exist either in the subsconscious mind or in dreams, which are its most easily recognizable by- product. There is no real past or future. It is like being eternally in the here and now. This is why traumas experienced in early childhood can affect people for years, even when their rational minds understand that they no longer have to worry about the past. This is also why we can pretend that something is true. The subconscious mind doesn't distinguish between truth and pretence when it is dealing with images unrelated to time.

FILL YOUR MIND WITH
THOUGHTS OF WEALTH

Your subconscious is like a vast field, governed, in a sense, by the "Law of Sowing", meaning that what you sow, you will reap. This universal law, which brooks no exceptions, has also been called the "Law of Compensation" by some authors. This law is to the mind what the law of cause and effect is to the physical world. Action breeds reaction. In the world of the mind, and so in life in general, thoughts and ideas are the cause; facts and events, the effect. Each thought that enters your mind tends to materialize in your life.

> All your thoughts tend to materialize in your life

This is why you must monitor your thoughts closely. If you continually think of your financial worries or never stop repeating that you can't make ends meet or that you might go bankrupt, you are entertaining thoughts that will show up in your life.

We certainly do not want to encourage recklessness. There is often a very fine line between lack of foresight and confidence, between optimism and brashness. We are not advocating a policy of burying your head in the sand like an ostrich, either. Difficulties and problems exist in any business dealing or enterprise. Nevertheless, billionaires, as well as hundreds of other millionaires, never let adversity defeat them. They no doubt saw the obstacles facing them, but their vision kept them going. They were inspired by dreams, which they constantly kept aflame. Instead of picturing only drawbacks and problems, they focused on the means they had to tackle and overcome them. Most people have more imagination when it comes to conjuring up problems that will prevent them from realizing their dreams than when it comes to recognizing their chances of success.

In the world of the mind, ideas really exist. Even if they are invisible, they are as real as the book you are holding in your hands or the chair you are sitting in. This is not an attempt to be mystical or to throw sand in your eyes. It has been said that ideas govern the world. The power they have is phenomenal. It is therefore necessary to constantly fill our minds with thoughts of abundance, richness, happiness and success. Each thought is a vibration, which, through some mysterious law of attraction, draws objects, being and circumstances of a similar nature to it. The negative attracts the negative in the same way that the positive attracts the positive.

FOLLOW YOUR DREAM UNTIL YOU MAKE A FORTUNE!

Daydreams are often sneered at by "down-to-earth" people who say that you have to look life squarely in the face and accept your fate, even if it leaves a lot to be desired. These are the kind of people who will systematically discourage progress and denigrate wealth, judging it to be vain and illusory. Yet, these resigned and unhappy individuals forget that there are two types of dreamers. On the one hand, there are daydreamers who make no attempt to turn their dreams into reality. On the other hand, there are "realistic" dreamers, who believe in the creative power of the subconscious. All artists have a mental picture of their future works of art. All politicians start out with plans to change society. All the successful sportsmen began by dreaming of their future success. But their dreams did not stop there. They took concrete measures to make them come true. Cristiano Ronaldo for instance practices football to an enormous extent to make him stay in form owing to facts that he is not as naturally gifted as Lionel Messi. Michael Jackson, continues to rake in millions every year despite his tragical death in 2009. It is almost impossible for any artist to come, to break his records of awards. This is because of the mental programming Michael did by saying " I will live forever through my music". A perfect example of the vibrations he emitted while alive.

Unfortunately, our educational system generally favour the rational and strictly logical part of thought, neglecting or even scorning its intuitive and imaginative side. Albert Einstein often quoted " Imagination is better than knowledge". This is because knowledge is the present state of the mind. Knowledge is where you exist now. It revolves around all logical and intellectual reasoning of your existence and co-existence with the universe. It can help you decide on your next course but it can never automatically place you on the next level. Only imagination can take you far from your current zone of existence. If you are not rich now, that is because you live in the knowledge of your present. The future in which you are rich comes only through imagination. Of course it does not happen overnight. You have to go through your own metamorphosis process at your own pace before you could fly in the air. The right side of the brain has always been considered second best. And yet, nothing great has ever been achieved without an original dream. A dream is a kind of projection of our inner selves. What, in fact, is a projection or a project? By definition, it is a part of us that we throw forward. The greater we programme our self-images to be, the more grandiose our dreams will be. And the most surprising thing is that a dream, however bold it may be, is often more easily attainable than we believe.

THE LABORATORY OF YOUR MIND

There is a very simple technique used by business people, artists and scientists to make use of the power of day-dreaming. Just as photographs are developed in a darkroom, you must develop your dreams in a dark-room. Sit or lie down in a room that you have made as dark and quiet as possible. Let images gradually flood your mind. Darkness and silence are particularly favourable for the growth of ideas and dreams because they put you in direct contact with your subconscious mind, which is essentially cut off from the outside world. It is important not to censure your thoughts, even if they seem far-fetched. This technique has been called 'brainstorming'. It can help you solve problems and discover a plethora of ideas.

YOUR SUBCONSCIOUS WILL LEAD
YOU INFALLIBLY TO WEALTH

The power of the subconscious is equaled only by its wisdom. It never forgets anything. It is the perfect registry of our lives, recording each and every one of our gestures, words and thoughts. Moreover, unlike the conscious mind, it never stops working. It works 24 hours a day. Filled with millions of events and ideas, your subconscious is a gold mine. It is equivalent to say that the subconscious mind is the DNA imprint of one thoughts. It attracts anything that you wish. Having said that it can attract problems if you keep a negative mindset. Emotions need to be well composed. Constant drowning in negative emotions destabilizes the mind. This in turn will destroy the construct of the subconscious mind. During a turbulent emotional state, whatever projection cease to take effect. Imagine placing a float on a turbulent sea. Eventually the float will disappear from sight and nowhere to be found. There goes your dream...

The only problem is that we often ignore it or don't dare to tap into it. But it's easy, and it's the best thing you could possibly do because all work without a good preliminary idea is pointless.

Your subconscious mind is the repository of thousands of ideas that could quickly make you rich. Yet, all you need is one. How do you find it? Learn how to converse with your subconscious. Send it a specific request, preferably at night before going to bed.

Earlier on we saw how important it was for your desires to be truly intense when you are formulating your suggestions. The same naturally goes for the requests you will send to your subconscious. The more vivid they are, the quicker they will be realized.

Rest assured, your subconscious will always provide you with the correct answer. The subconscious, if you remember, is where all our impressions, thoughts, and actions are registered. But what is more fascinating still is that it has access to information that we have never recorded, and therefore to things that we do not know about. This principle is illustrated in our own lives, if we think about it for a minute, as well as in the lives of the wealthy. Steven Spielberg once had a film project in mind as well as a scenario. All he needed was a producer, which is often the case in the field of motion picture. One day, while he was on the beach, he 'accidentally' met a rich man who was ready to invest in young film makers. With the money Spielberg received form this producer, a total stranger to him, he was able to shoot *Amblin,* which was given an Honourable Mention at the Venice Film Festival and drew attention to him in Hollywood. Michael Jackson collaborating with Quincy Jones in the production of Thriller, the best selling album of all time was not pre-mediated. You may say these people had talent, they have a base to take on. What do I have? But let me tell you, there are millions of people out there who has got talent and they went undiscovered forever. There are also people with lesser talent who made it extremely huge. I don't know about you, but I would choose to be in the second category all the way.

This if often how your subconscious solves a problem. You will meet someone 'by chance' who will help you put your plan into action. You will just happen to read a newspaper article or book or see a TV programme that will provide a clear-cut answer to something puzzling you or to a problem holding you back.

Those who remain unaware of or ignore this principle generally state that these happy coincidences are the result of luck or fate. Yet in a world physically and mentally governed by the law of cause and effect, *fate does not exist*. The same goes for good and bad luck, which are actually the unexpected and often belated consequences of two things: our thoughts and previous actions.

However, if your mind has been programmed that, fate or luck is an integral part of human life, then you can re-program it by saying, destiny will take care of 10% of my life's journey and I am in charge of 90% of the outcomes, you certainly fall on the safe side. Based on my research, communities or people in country that believe in astrology and fortune-telling often are less industrious than people living elsewhere who believe in their own capacity. List out ten successful people of the world that you admire and point out how many actually believed in fate or fortune-telling. All would have believed in fame and fortune nevertheless.

Personally I would say acquiring knowledge of any field does not create harm. It is the limitation and restriction, plus the extent to which this knowledge weakens the mind is what really matters. Superstitious people are one example. These people are carrying extra burdens in their lives in the name of fate, luck, superstition, astrology and the likes. You need to give your subconscious mind the freedom to operate at the field of infinite possibilities. Only then the results will flow in with effortless ease. Setting a high goal and also creating doubt and fear in the mind would certainly lead to a standstill in your projects. As long you have the right set of attitude, a loving heart filled with generosity, nothing can stop you from thriving! The arms of the Universal Mind will open, light will lit your pathway and blessings will shower!

Eradication of feelings of jealousy, being humble as well being emphatical of the lives of others will turbo-boost your journey to success. You may argue that rich people are ruthless and they are ready to ruin other is a false belief. Thinking in such way itself is an indication that you carry a narrow-minded perspective of the rich and it will be your own downfall to attain wealth. If you know someone who is rich but does not have the true rich-man's mindset. His downfall is certain. There are millions of millionaires have turned bankrupt overnight. There are millions others who manage to hold on to their wealth, but they could be lacking what other rich people have. Happiness. The true rich are the ones who forsakes the abundance lifestyle but cultivates the affluence mindset.

Anyone who adequately programmes his subconscious, that is to say, permeates it with positive thoughts of fame and fortune, and who tirelessly attempts to realize his dreams, will eventually reach his goal.

In a sense, we literally make our own good and bad luck. This is why we can say without hesitation that the people who learn and apply the laws of the mind and of success correctly can forge their own destinies.

If you start applying these universal laws today, you will soon discover that you are not creating your success alone. Your circle of family and friends and, at the same time, the strangers you meet will also contribute to your success. One example of this principle is the way Steven Spielberg got the idea for his first successful film *Duel*. It was not the result of long cogitations or intensive research. Far from it,. One day his secretary suggested he read a short story in a magazine. When he read it, Spielberg was ecstatic. He knew immediately that he had found the idea he was looking for. Without his secretary, he probably would never have fallen upon this breathtaking story. But his subconscious was there, taking care of everything. Needless to say, "lucky strokes" such as this one are commonplace not only in the lives of the rich, but everyone. The only difference is the less richer often fail to create a platform on par with the rich, by not putting enough initiative in the subconscious mind's registry.

Not only does everything the rich touch turn to gold, but all the people they meet help them get richer. The same can happen to you. Make use of your subconscious mind. It is there to serve you.

We could go on and on about the unimaginable powers of the subconscious and the way to make use of it, but there are already hundreds of books devoted to this subject. In any case, you now possess the key principles that will allow you to succeed and enrich yourself according to your ambition and self-image. We shall now discover how to fulfill one of the capital requirements of success: *making the right decision.*

MAKING THE RIGHT DECISION

As we see in everyday lives most milionaires and billionaires are people of unshakeable faith and conviction, enabling them to conquer all the obstacles blocking their path to fame and fortune. Faith is one of the keys to success. A survey of the lives of several millionaires carried out at the request of the billionaire Andrew Carnegie allowed Napoleon Hill, the author of *Think and Grow Rich,* to state that the supreme secret of success is faith: the human mind can accomplish whatever it believes in.

Faith in yourself and in what you do is therefore vital. All successful people believe implicitly in their dreams. Nothing seems impossible to them.

Having faith is one thing, you will probably object, but how do you know whether you are putting it into a good idea and not making a disastrous mistake? Besides, even millionaires and seasoned businessmen make costly mistakes. Isn't it even more dangerous for someone just starting out? How so you know how to separate the chaff from the wheat? How can you decide what is possible or not? How can you find an idea, plan, or job that you can fully believe in? In other words, how can you develop the type of sound judgement that allows you to reduce, if not eliminate, mistakes?

We are constantly called upon to make decisions. This might involve accepting or looking for a new job, choosing a career, backing a project, or making an investment. Anyone wishing to survive and grow rich must make the right decision as often as possible. Is there a surefire method of developing this ability? Yes, there is!

This ability will help you discover what to believe in, which will enable you to be successful. Things that are too obvious rarely allow us get rich. If this were the case, everybody would be wealthy. Anyone who manages to make a fortune, while those around him wallow in mediocrity, tighten their belts and make do with what they have, is comparable to a clairvoyant amidst the blind. Unlike most people, successful people have acquired the capacity to perceive possibilities, even when things seem impossible. They see beyond the obstacles blocking their paths. They recognize the means that will ultimately lead them to victory.

Succeeding in business or in a career means walking a tightrope. A wrong move, while not necessarily fatal, does mean a temporary setback. We must therefore learn how to make right decisions more often than wrong ones. This means knowing how to say "yes" when the time is ripe, "no" when it isn't, and avoiding shaky business deals at all costs.

It is encouraging to note that most wealthy men do not believe that this ability is inborn, but that it can be acquired and enhanced, meaning that it is accessible to anyone who takes the time and energy to obtain and cultivate it. This chapter will explain how. Learning this fundamental skill is much easier than you would imagine.

The greater your capacity to see possibilities where others see only impossibilities and to make the right decisions, the more of an eccentric people will take you for. Most people tend to reject good opportunities when they knock at the door. Once you have ventured on to the road to success, do your best to ignore those who criticize you or throw snide comments your way.

The objections raised by the people around us, as well as by experts, are admittedly founded on " rational" analyses. It is by cultivating our intuition that we can manage to see beyond "logical" ideas. Besides, the secret of success lies in being able to distinguish between what is feasible and what is not, and in finding a vein of gold where others can't see it.

True, it would be naïve to claim that absolutely everything under the sun is possible. Some plans are simply not viable or would require too much time or energy. The bestseller *What They Don't Teach You at Harvard Business School* supplies an amusing example of this principle.

A dog food company was holding its annual sales convention. During the course of the convention the president of the company listened patiently as his advertising director introduced a point-of-sale scheme that would "revolutionize the industry", and his sales director extolled the virtues of "the best damn sales force in the business". Finally it was time for the president to go to the podium and make his closing remarks.

"Over the past few days," he began, "we've heard from all our division heads of their wonderful plans for the coming year. Now as we draw to a close, I have only one question. If we have the best advertising, the best marketing, the best sales force, how come we sell less goddamn dog food than anyone in the business?"

Absolute silence filled the convention hall. Finally, after what seemed like forever, a small voice answered from the back of the room: "Because the dogs hate it."

Although this is an amusing anecdote, it proves that there are more possibilities than impossibilities. All you need to do is think of most inventions, for examples. Did you know that when the Wright brothers were inventing their plane, scientific studies were undertaken to demonstrate that anybody heavier than air couldn't possibly fly?

Soichiro Honda's life story exemplifies the same principle. His autobiography includes the following eloquent passage on this subject:

When I started manufacturing motorcycles, prophets of doom, who were sometimes my best friends, came to discourage me. "Why don't you simply set up a garage? You'd rake in tons of money. There are lots of cars to repair all over the country." I didn't listen to their pessimistic advice; so, beside my research laboratory, I started up the Honda Motor Company on September 24, 1948. It now covers the entire world.

Honda, a typical optimist, was able to see possibilities where others were blind, and to jump into action regardless of the negative arguments raised against his idea. Explaining his decision, he goes on to say:

> We were extremely poor, with our meager capital of one million yen, but hard-working and very aware of the enormous risks we were taking. We were hoping to raise an industrial sector out of the doldrums at a time when the national industry lay destroyed before us. We were taking the absurd gamble of selling motorcycles when people were too poor at that moment to buy petrol and, if the economic situation got better, would later on surely want to own cars. We were flying in the face of even the most optimistic economic forecasts.

This is a clear illustration of the predominance of mind over matter and of optimism over pessimism. People with a positive mental attitude apparently tell themselves that things are never as bad as they look at first, and will always end up being even better.

One day during the Second World War, an American was taking a photograph of his young daughter when she asked him why they had to wait to see the picture—a naïve, even absurd, question, but one which particularly interested her farther. Her father was Edwin H. Land, an inventor who had already made improvements to the camera. His daughter's candid question started him thinking seriously about this matter. His Reasoning Was AS Follows: Someone who buys a pair of trousers or car, or any commodity for that matter, can use it immediately after buying it. Why should it be any different in photography? Why should you have to wait days or even weeks to see the pictures you have taken? But would it be possible to develop photos in a tiny closed-off space in a matter of seconds when it normally took hours in a professional laboratory? All of Land's scientist friends told him his plan was impossible. Six months after his daughter's ingenuous question, the problem was resolved-in theory. On November 26 1948, the first 60-second Polaroid camera went on sale in Boston. As soon as the store opened, customers stampeded to get their hands on one of them.

A little girl's spontaneous remark instigated the invention of the Polaroid camera. Because children's minds are not yet filled with prejudices and preconceived notions, they have the ability to view things with a fresh eye and to see possibilities where rational minds see only impossibilities. In fact, genius has long been considered 'childhood revisited'. Prejudices have little or no hold on the minds of geniuses, who manage to hang on their spark of originality, or at least find it again, through long and determined efforts. Traditional education is a handicap in a sense, as we shall see later on in this book. Excessive analysis, skepticism and an overly critical eye lead to mental stagnation and paralysis. Analytical studies are by definition interminable. Few millionaire men, went to university. Many were dropouts. It was to some extent their 'ignorance' that helped them preserve their derring-do and enthusiasm, a point we shall have the opportunity to come back to.

**The key to success is seeing possibilities
where others see only impossibilities**

This principle applies not only to inventions and large-scale enterprises, but to smaller endeavours as well. How often have you seen people raise their eyebrows at one of your seemingly impossible schemes? How often have you judged something unlikely or a job inaccessible to you before realizing that just the opposite was true?

Because of 'rationality' or more often a secret lack of confidence, we give up our dreams, consoling ourselves with the thought that it wouldn't have worked out anyway. If you think this over for a minute, you will realize that this problem is intimately linked with our self-image. It is possible to categorically state that the better your self-image is, the more likely you will be able to see that a range of possibilities exists. There is a direct ratio between them.

It should be added, however, that many plans and ideas are neither feasible nor unfeasible, but somewhere between the two. What makes the difference between success and failure when putting them into action is the quantity and quality of the energy invested in them. They come to life and become viable through the sheer force of the vitality and thought put into them.

A person with a healthy ego is a powerhouse of energy and can easily tap into the unlimited reserves of his subconscious. Consequently, not only is he able to discern the positive side of things more easily, but his energy enables him to turn it to his advantage.

> **To gain a clearer vision of what is possible, expand your self-image**

The major flaw of those who hesitate about carrying out a plan is trying to identify all the obstacles they could eventually run up against and ignoring the tools they have at their disposal to combat them – a paralyzing, anxiety-producing attitude if ever there was one! Thus, the appropriate attitude to adopt is to look for all the reasons you are likely to succeed instead of conjuring up all the stumbling blocks you might face. You must, of course, weigh all the pros and cons. What happens in many cases, however, is that despite 10 favourable reasons, all it takes is one negative one to discourage people from trying at all. The reason for this is simple: most people are programmed negatively. Based on the principle of attraction, positive arguments, no matter how numerous they are, don't find fertile ground in a mind programmed negatively, whereas a single obstacle thrives there at once.

At this very moment, thousands of people are rejecting perfectly good ideas, plans and dreams because a single negative idea has paralysed their judgement.

Naturally, it is extremely important to find out as much as possible beforehand about a proposed business deal, job offer, or plan. But remember, there are always imponderables in the end. Even the most detailed and sophisticated analyses will not dispel the unknown completely. Furthermore, studies undertaken by corporations and individuals alike often end up confirming their original ideas. Every scheme, admittedly, implies change and the need to confront the unknown. Psychological studies have demonstrated that people are frightened by unexplored territory and view change as a threat, or at least as cause for anxiety.

It is important, even essential, to know the facts before making a decision, but it should be recalled that facts must not take the place of intuition, an ability you must learn to cultivate. You must also discover how to interpret facts, for facts and figures in themselves do not constitute a conclusion. It is up to you to draw your own conclusion from the data you have collected.

DO IT NOW!

The fundamental weakness that ruins so many people's lives is procrastination. It goes without saying that time is often a vital component of any dream or scheme. An idea that came to nothing at any given time could be valid in six months or a year. A phone call might work wonders at one moment instead of another. Nevertheless, the best decision is to do it now. All wealthy people have shown the remarkable ability to make rapid-fire decisions. Even in matters involving big money, they acted much faster than we realize. All things being relative, you might object that the sums they were playing around with, considerable in the eyes of most common mortals, were a pittance to them. This is not the case, however. Their on-the-spot decisions were often made at the beginning of their careers putting their entire fortunes, meager back then, on the line. One of those whose success largely depended on the ability to come to a speedy decision was Conrad Hilton. While still young, Hilton vaguely thought of becoming a banker. Heeding his friend's advice to check out banking possibilities in Texas, he went to San Francisco and happened to see a hotel which he was thinking about buying. Years later, a reporter from *Nation's Business* asked:

> "So....you looked at the books and decided this was a good proposition. Right?"
> "I saw that it was much better than baking. I hadn't taken over the hotel 24 hour before I decided,"
> "This is what I am going to do. This is my life."
> "Your mind was set from then?"
> "Right there, I made up my mind. I didn't want anything else. That was in 1919. Certainly the banker raising the price $5,000 steered me off banking. But what really did it was going over there and seeing the bustle, having the owner tell me about all the business that he was doing, how the trains were coming in there at night and the money he was making. When he showed me the books, I figured that I could get all of my money back in one year,"

Notice that Hilton had made up his mind before the owner had even shown him the books. This will surely rile all those who advocate long feasibility studies! It should nevertheless be mentioned that Hilton had seen the hotel and been struck by its extraordinary opulence.

Hilton started out in business with the paltry sum of $5,000, including $3,000 from his inheritance and $2,000 in savings. By purchasing this hotel, he was gambling every penny he had. Making a decision out of the blue like this is comparable to falling in love at first sight. Besides Hilton, many other millionaires have experienced this kind of "instant love" throughout their careers. It wouldn't even be stretching the truth to say that they wouldn't make a decision without it. These men, who were so persuasive when convinced of something never let their advisers, friends, or facts and figures change their minds. Often they followed advice only if it confirmed their initial ideas. It should be mentioned, however, that their stubbornness did betray them at times, making them lose a lot of money. Despite this, their determination made them heed their inner voices, and this was one of the determining factors in their success.

In the case mentioned above, Hilton had seen the small hotel's potential rather than its current productivity. At the same time he had a mental picture of how to make it produce a profit. This is how he explained it in the same interview:

> I saw around the hotel, we were not getting what we should out of the space. So I changed it and I have kept that as a rule throughout my life, to find out what is the best use I could make of space. You see, you can either lose your money or you can make it, depending upon whether you know what the public wants. You have to know that and give them the most space available.
>
> I figured out that customers at the Mobley (Hotel in San Francisco) could get food someplace else, and that they didn't need the hotel dining room. So we put beds in there. We were making no money on the food, and the rooms were in terrific demand. Today you might find that the best use of space is in a restaurant.
>
> Another thing was building *esprit de corps* among the help. We got all the employees together and told them that they were largely responsible for whether the guests of the hotel were pleased and would ever come back. I have done that throughout my life.

Hilton made snap judgements throughout his life, and his optimism and boldness were rewarded more often than not. Instead of harping on the obstacles preventing him from financing his schemes, he told himself that he would find a way around them. And he did!

The lives many millionaires studied, reveals that all of them at one point or another had to burn their bridges behind them, cutting off all retreat. This usually involved giving up a job offer without knowing what lay in store for them or investing all of their money in some venture or other. In either case, failure would be catastrophic. It was do or die!

Honda illustrates this principle in his autobiography. After having been a somewhat successful industrialist, he encountered technical problems so great that he had to hit the books again at the University of Hamasatsu when he was over 30 years old. He wasn't able to produce a piston flexible enough to function in an engine. Here is what he had to say about this:

> Every morning from then on I went to school and, at night, put everything I had learned during the day into practice. I forced myself to be enthusiastic because I had no choice in the matter. And yet, when you put yourself in situations with only one alternative, you get a new feeling of freedom: making a decision that you can't back down from. A thousand reasons crossed my mind to justify why I had to keep on going. My friends and above all, my father, but also the employees working for me, all had faith in me. I no longer had the right to turn back, and school was the only way I had to overcome this situation, to become a real engineer capable of doing engineering jobs, to discover the theories behind my technical intuitions and to put them into practice. I solemnly told myself: "If I give up now, everyone will die of hunger." And I pictured in my mind the poor, pathetic people who depended on me.

Why is the technique of putting your back to the wall and cutting off all your exits so effective? We have already seen that you can submit specific requests to your subconscious and even give it orders to a certain extent. We also mentioned that, to get a speedy response, your desires, dreams, and ambitions have to be felt intensely. By burning all your bridges behind you, your wishes become much more imperative, thereby activating your instinct to survive. This in turn produces results so great that people, unaware of this principle, come to wonder whether successful individuals are gifted with the ability to influence the outcome of events!

By making a snap decision and scorning the obstacles he might possibly confront, Hilton puts himself in a do-or-die situation, cutting off all his exits, and results followed almost miraculously. He, of course, started out with a positive mental programme. His subconscious was clearly directed towards success. Moreover, he depended on his intuition, an ability which is simply the special capacity to enter into contact with a positive subconscious mind. Besides, what else is a flash of inspiration, but a sudden revelation of the subconscious which means that the external object, opportunity or deal (in Hilton's case, a small hotel) matches a specific type of programming exactly? In other words, Conrad Hilton had programmed his subconscious to make a fortune. His conscious mind (whose power is limited, as we have seen) wanted him to buy a bank. He even had the opportunity and financial backing of a friend to do so. But his subconscious, which knew what was good for him, realized that he was destined to become a brilliant hotel operator and led him to that small hotel. His intuitive response was, as always, the conscious revelation of what was registered in his subconscious. This coincidental encounter between the subconscious and its external manifestation sparks excitement and enthusiasm.

This is why you will always be able to rely on your sixth sense as soon as you have learned how to programme your subconscious. This ability, the cornerstone of success, will increasingly develop as you learn how to make good use of this part of your mind. It will even become second nature to you in the long run. You will soon be able to command the most powerful computer of all – the subconscious mind. It will enable you to make faster and more reliable decisions. Haste hinders good counsel, so the proverb goes. There is undoubtedly a grain of truth in this, and yet procrastination and slowness surely do more wrong than hasty decisions. If these rich men erred on the side of excess, it was in making snap decisions. But that was how they got rich.

But how is it possible to know when to make a decision? How do you know whether you have examined the situation enough and have all the necessary facts at your disposal? The answer is to rely on your subconscious. Programme it by repeating: "My subconscious immediately gives me the right answer."

Sleep is the mother of counsel. Nothing rings truer than this old adage because we can easily contact our subconscious at night. So, sleep on your problem. Write all the facts you know about it, listing all the pros and cons. This might seem obvious to you, but this technique is invaluable for clearing up doubt. If the scale tips in favour of one side at first, your decision will be easy. If the pros and cons balance out, let your subconscious deal with it. It will come to you with an answer – the right one!

WHY NOT TOSS A COIN?

You probably think this is a joke, but hang on a moment. This is merely a small trick to help you make contact with your subconscious. Of course, you must determine yourself what each side of the coin represents. Flip a coin right now. Keep a close eye on your reactions. If heads shows up, telling you to go ahead with your plan, and you are disappointed, it's probably because your subconscious doesn't really believe in it. If tails appears, it is a vital clue that you do not trust your plan and have already made up your mind without realizing it. There are four possible reactions in this game, two of which we have already described. In each case, analyse your reactions well. Don't consider the results you get as definite, but only as a means of helping you come to a decision. Experience has shown that this trivial little game often helps resolve a matter one way or another, usually for the better, especially when the pros and cons are split 50-50.

Let us add a further point: when the pros and cons balance out that evenly, it's perhaps a sign that your plan will run up against many problems or that it will not be completely successful. What is certain, however, is that the doubt persisiting in your mind is a bad omen. It could eventually undermine your enthusiasm and faith. Since you only half-way believe in it already, the results you get will be in keeping with your expectations. We have already seen the importance that faith and enthusiasm have. If your plan doesn't fire you up enough, it would be best to discard it for another. The richest men often got involved only in projects they believed in 100 per cent, and they started out totally confident in their ultimate success.

Once you have learned how to make snap decisions and come face to face with a problem that makes you hesitate too long, beware. It could very well be the sign of an unsound proposition. This is another reason why speedy decisions are a good omen, even if the answer is "no". Making quick decisions is also knowing how to say "no" quickly. This is not necessarily the product of a pessimistic mind, but only that not everything under the sun is valid, otherwise everybody would be a millionaire. However, if you systematically say "no" to everything and never undertake anything for fear of making a mistake, it is an indication that you are poorly programmed.

Another reason why it is preferable to make hasty decisions is that good opportunities don't last forever. You must grab them while they're hot. New ones will of course knock at your door, but if you hesitate every time, you will miss out on every one of them. Hesitation can be fatal. You are not the only one in the race. If a sound opportunity crops up, remember that many others will see it too. Some of the vital facts will still be missing of course. But if you wait until you have your hands on all of them, chances are you will let the opportunity slip through your fingers.

This is what often happens to those who prefer analysing everything instead of trusting their intuition, the profound wisdom of their subconscious. Furthermore, proponents of long, in-depth analyses are inclined to forget that situations change all the time, and when they are finally ready to act, the facts they have are no longer relevant, thus their decisions are right off the mark.

In his autobiography, Lee Iacocca, who saved Chrysler from bankruptcy, makes an interesting point on this subject:

> nothing stands still in this world. I like to go duck hunting, where constant movement and change are facts of life. You can aim at a duck and get it in your sights, but the duck is always moving. *In order to hit the duck, you have to move your gun.* But a committee faced with a major decision can't always move as quickly as the events it's trying to respond to. By the time the committee is ready to shoot, the duck has flown away.

Those who take too long to make up their minds often land in the same position as this clumsy hunter. As the old saying goes, "Fortune favours the bold".

TAKE A BREAK

We have just proved the necessity of making speedy decisions. Despite their boldness and daring, many successful men have developed the habit of thinking things over one last time before taking the plunge. This "time out" might last an hour, a few minutes, or even seconds. When you take this last-minutes breather, go over all the arguments one by one. Verify the logic behind them and the way you arrived at your conclusion. Don't forget to write them down if you haven't done it yet. Writing is like using a developer in photography – without it, getting a clear picture is impossible. Then, set yourself a deadline and stop mulling your problem over. Tell yourself that in one hour, at exactly 3 p.m., for example, you will make your decision.

Better yet, sleep on it. Before falling asleep, go over all the facts and then hand them over to your subconscious to untangle. Your position will often be much clearer in the morning.

IS IT NECESSARY TO WAIT FOR THE IDEAL TIME?

The ideal time doesn't exist. It's a figment of the imagination of those who believe it exists. Most people make the mistake of waiting around for it. It's a perfect excuse, which people claim to be serious, well thought-out, the logical decision. Generally speaking, the ideal time is now. Right away. If you want to succeed, start today, this very minute.

STICK TO YOUR DECISION

One of the characteristic tendencies of the rich is that they stick to their decisions come hell or high water, regardless of everybody else's opinions, or of circumstances, obstacles, past failure or temporary setbacks.

Blindly adhering to your first option makes a lot of plans fall through. But sticking to your final decision is being logical with yourself and confirms your inner certainty that you have aimed right on target. Those who constantly change their minds will never be successful. Vacillation is a sign of a mental state gnawed by doubt. Since we have clearly seen that circumstances always end up duplicating our inner thoughts, there can be no question that doubt leads straight to failure. Consequently, success depends on two vital factors:

> 1. **Making snap decisions**
> 2. **Sticking to them and jumping straight into action**

HOW FAR SHOULD YOU STICK TO YOUR DECISION?

The principle of firmly upholding your decision is a general one, meaning that there are exceptions to the rule. Blindly adhering to a decision, come what may, implies that people never go wrong. Now, everybody, including the most astute entrepreneurs, makes mistakes and wrong decisions. It is therefore vital to be wary of being overly rigid and theoretical. We must learn to adapt to circumstances. One of the keys to success is finding the delicate balance between persistence and flexibility.

Sticking to your initial decision at all costs could be fatal to your success. Bet most people fail because they give up much too quickly.

An engineer called Mr Head had to do forty-three tests, spread out over three long years before he found a successful way of making a metal ski. If he had given up after his forty-second try, the metal ski would still have been invented and made someone a millionaire, but not Head.

Look around to see how widespread the tendency is to give up too quickly. What about you? How many times have you thrown in the towel after one or two failures? Have you ever persisted in what you were doing without getting discouraged after experiencing two failures in a row? All too often pride or a lack of self-confidence makes people give up too soon. Worse yet, they comfort themselves selves by saying that it was to be expected anyway. This does not mean that someone with a positive mental programme will not suffer defeat. All great success stories are punctuated with failures. The difference between positive and negative people is that the former will not let themselves be beaten down by their first blunders. If they don't succeed the first time, they always try, try again.

The lives of the richest men in the world have revealed a somewhat mysterious phenomenon. Life seems to have been designed as a test. When people have shown they could overcome obstacles and failures with unswerving calmness and faith, Life appears to lay down her weapons, in a manner of speaking, and fame and fortune appear, as if charmed by the strength of these people. Honda offered a similar observation in his life story:

> A company laboratory seems to be the best learning centre for mistakes! In fact, most researchers recognize that 99 per cent of the time they are dealing with hopeless cases. The modest percentage that survives this … is nonetheless enough to justify their efforts. Finally, I myself do not regret the thousands of times I have come home without a catch, having lost all of my bait and tackle. When days become this dark and gloomy, it means that the treasure I am looking for is about to be discovered. The great flash of light and hope that burst forth make me instantly forget my long hours of tedious work.

Napoleon Hill supports this opinion in one of his books, in which he relates that success often follows a resounding failure as if life wanted to reward the brave soul able to surmount such a devastating setback.

Determination, a quality absent in most people, is often generously rewarded. It must not, however, be confused with blind pigheadedness. The authors of *In Search of Excellence* conducted an experiment to illustrate the fact that we must watch out for dogmatism and stubbornness and learn how to adapt to circumstances (one of the secrets behind the success of the one hundred companies studied in the analysis).

'… If you place in a bottle half a dozen bees and the same number of flies, and lay the bottle down horizontally with its base to the window, you will find that the bees will persist, till they die of exhaustion or hunger, in their endeavor to discover an issue through the glass, while the flies, in less than two minutes, will all have sallied forth through the neck on the opposite side… It is their (the bees) love of light, it is their very intelligence, that is their undoing in this experiment. They evidently imagine that the issue from every prison must be there where the light shines clearest; and they act in accordance, and persist in too logical action. To them, glass is a supernatural mystery they never have met in nature; they have had no experience of this suddenly impenetrable atmosphere; and, the greater their intelligence, the more inadmissible, more incomprehensible, will the strange obstacle appear. Whereas the feather-brained flies, careless of logic as of the enigma of crystal, disregarding the call of the light, flutter wildly hither and thither, and meeting here the good fortune that often waits on the simple, who find salvation there where the wiser will perish, necessarily end by discovering the friendly opening that restores their liberty to them.

It has thus been demonstrated that in business the ability to adapt quickly is one of the keys to success and that pragmatism and trial and error are better than idealism and dogmatism. But how do you know whether to persevere like the bees in the above-mentioned experiment or to change course to gain your freedom, your success? It would seem that the best, and possibly only, means is relying on a well-programmed subconscious. It will tell you when to keep at it, when to review your position, and when to adopt a plan better than your initial one. If you hit upon a short-cut to success after discovering new facts or following the advice of a friend, take it. You must learn to adapt your decisions to achieve even greater success. Making a new snap decision or changing your mind can often save a situation.

Mistakes will be made all the same. The best attitude to adopt with respect to blunders is the one shared by those who made it big in the past. You must abhor making mistakes before the fact. However, you must not take for granted that you will make them before you do. This breeds passivity and submissiveness. You must accept them after having made them. This is what successful people do. Once again, **TAKE ACTION!** Regardless of the ever-present possibility of going wrong, the law of numbers favours those who make many attempts. The ideal situation would be to minimize the incidence of miscarried attempts. Successful ones will largely compensate for occasional flops whether you are searching for a job, starting up a company, or launching a product. Frankly, what is it to you if you get five doors slammed in your face when the sixth one opens up with an exciting prospect, offering you what you have been looking for all the time: the perfect job?

LEARN TO FORGET YOUR FAILURES!

One of the most indispensable skills to acquire on the road to riches is the subtle art of forgetting your failures and turning towards the future. Those who cannot do this are often paralysed by the spectre of past mistakes. They literally live in the past and fear the future. This is really too bad. They believe that because they failed once or twice or 10 times they are talentless or unlucky.

The rich all went through this, but it didn't stop them in their tracks. You must not look back or linger over the past. Life is ahead of you. Go for it!

LEARN FROM YOUR MISTAKES!

Each failure is a lesson unto itself. It has been said that people learn more from their failures than from their successes. They put themselves into question, analyse their ideas, methods and concepts, and benefit from this experience. There is no shame in making a mistake. What is generally a waste is making the same mistake twice. Straighten out your ideas about failure. If you have thoughtfully reasoned out why you failed, you will gain a clearer understanding of how to succeed. In this sense, each failure leads you closer to success. This is not only a paradox, but a truth, as witnessed by the experience of those already become super rich men.

All you have to do is to acknowledge the philosopher Bergson's motto: "Act like a man of thought; think like a man of action."

THE BEST WAY TO GROW RICH

"I would have liked to have set up my own business, but I didn't have the talent or skills I thought it required."

'My dream was to become a writer, but my father disapproved; so, I became a civil servant.'

'My job bores me to tears, but there's so much unemployment that I'd better not kid myself about finding a new one.'

'I used to dream of being a lawyer, but I didn't think I had what it takes to get through law school; so, I decided to do something else.'

How often have you heard avowals such as these, or variations on the same theme? How often have you yourself had similar muddled thoughts? Out of every 10 people, how many can boast of really enjoying their jobs? They are few and far between, in fact. Unfortunately, most people simply don't like what they do. The most tragic thing about all of this is that they are convinced that their hands are tied, that they will never be able to change their situations; in other words, that fate has permanently sentenced them to a life of mediocrity and drudgery.

If you find yourself in this position and dislike your job, which only frustrates you, think about the following question: don't you find it sad and even tragic that you will die without ever having done what you really want to do? Aren't you worth more than that? Don't you think that society has tricked and cheated you by preventing you from doing what pleases you?

Take a typical day in your life. You work eight hours, doing a job you hate, then sleep eight hours. This leaves you with another eight hours, eight miserable hours that you use to recover, trying to forget the frustrations heaped on you during your day. What kind of life is this? A pretty sad one, don't you think? And yet, you keep on doing it, believing you must.

This passive, fatalistic view is wrong. Nothing obliges you to keep working at a job you don't like. You can do something about it. There is a job for you that can impassion you as much as, if not more than, your current one. And you could start doing it right now. Immediately. This is not an empty promise. Why not get started as you read these words? Is life so poorly designed that it is meant to frustrate you constantly and deprive you of what you truly want? Impossible! Life is not that bad. It gives you exactly what your faith and self-image expect.

Life gives you exactly what you expect from it

What prevents most people from getting what they want is that they believe it is impossible. According to the principles stated previously, they get exactly what they expect from life: boredom, frustration, obstacles, and low incomes. People are what they believe themselves to be.

Think about your life as it is and especially how you picture it to be. If you are not doing what you would like to be doing (as can be normally expected), look back on your life. Make a list right now of six reasons supporting your belief that you cannot do what truly pleases you.

1...
2...
3...
4...
5...
6...

Now go over your list point by point and think about each reason you have written down. Are these obstacles really valid? Whatever they are (excluding a severe mental handicap or illiteracy, both improbable in this case, since you wouldn't be reading this book), there is no way that they can stand up to a serious and realistic analysis. Let us stress the word realistic, since people generally tend to accuse legitimate ambitions of being 'unrealistic'.

Denying our personal inclinations and ambitions normally begins very early in life. Yet, to be happy and self-fulfilled, we must be courageous enough to be ourselves. You have allowed yourself to be thwarted and have denied your inner self in the name of conformity for far too long. This is a mistake, but fortunately, nothing is irreversible.

As you analysed your list of reasons, you might have noticed that they are the same ones preventing you from getting rich. The relationship between the two is no coincidence. In fact, we can establish the following basic principle, which will probably surprise you: to make money, lots of it, you must first do what you enjoy in life. The reason is simple. If you don't enjoy your work, you cannot do it well: this is an absolute principle. When your heart isn't in something, you experience a drastic slump in energy and motivation. You inevitably come up with mediocre results or at least with a much poorer performance than if you loved what you were doing. It follows as a rule of thumb that your boss, associates, or clients, whatever the case may be, cannot be 100 per cent satisfied with what you accomplish.

If you are an employee, the chances are low that you will get promoted to a more interesting position or receive a substantial rise. If you are in business, the chances are high that your firm will not flourish. The monetary rewards you get will reflect this. When you receive poor compensation for your work, your motivation plummets and the quality of your work with it. It's a vicious circle!

Furthermore, people rarely work alone. If you hate your job, your enthusiasm is low, and you will drag your colleagues down with you. This is why one of the fundamental keys to success is to do what you enjoy doing.

Mark McCormack, the author of that excellent book, *What They Don't Teach You at Harvard Bussiness School,* comments on job dissatisfaction, emphasizing this point :

> Boredom occurs when the learning curve flattens out.
> It can happen to anyone at any level of the corporation. In fact, it occurs most often in successful people who need more challenge and stimulation than do others.
> One of the sure signs of incipient boredom is knowing your job too well, or knowing all the right buttons to push. I simply will not allow this to happen to myself.
> I find that I am redefining my job all the time, taking on new tasks, or constantly creating new challenges for myself. If I reach some goal, either personal or corporate, that goal immediately becomes a step in the learning process toward another, more ambitious goal.
> This, I believe, is how people grow in their jobs and grow in importance to their company.

He then argues forcefully:

> If you're bored it's your fault. You just aren't working hard enough at making your job interesting. It is also probably the reason you haven't been offered anything better. Find out what you love to do and you will be successful at it.

When we declare that you must love your work, in no way are we suggesting that your ideal job will be devoid of frustration, disappointment, and problems. It won't necessarily be heaven on earth every day. But it's a little like true love. The deep bonds linking two people make them forget or overcome the short-lived dilemmas and obstacles that crop up along the way.

Some people don't really know whether they like their jobs or not. Admittedly, many wealthy men, who unanimously loved their work, went through temporary, but very real, periods of discouragement, depression and even self-doubt. If you want to find out if you really love your work, we propose that you take this little test, which is simple, but highly effective if you answer honestly:

> **If you won a million dollars, would**
> **you stay in your present job**

If your answer is 'yes', congratulations! You obviously like what you do. Most millionaires would have answered in the affirmative. Their lives prove that their work was their passion. Many of them not only made a million dollars, but several hundred millions...

When talking about the very rich, people who are poor and often hate their jobs to boot, often say: 'If I were in their shoes, I'd stop working and travel around the world.' They don't seem to understand that, even if money is an important consideration in the lives of the rich, what really goads them into action is loving their work and constantly desiring to do new things, to take up new challenges, and to face new risks.

This is why the rich rarely take holidays. True, their numerous obligations often preclude their taking time off, but the real reason is that work is their passion. For them, working is a pleasure, a leisure activity. This is also why they often work late into the night and don't hesitate to put in 15 or 18-hour days.

Rest assured, working so hard didn't kill them. Far from it. Besides, if you read the news most super rich men lived to a ripe old age and some worked until just before their deaths. Retirement made no sense to them. What a contrast between them and those whose sole ambition is to retire and who rejoice over 'liberal' policies recommending 'early retirement'. Those people have withdrawn from life and forgotten who they are. They are part of the 'living dead'.

If you want to live a long and happy life, do what you enjoy doing. One of the principle causes of ageing is stress and frustration. To stay eternally young inside, you must respect your heart's desires and do what you enjoy.

Steven Spielberg once said: 'The worst thing this notoriety can bring. . . is to make me lazy.' He was joking, no doubt. Despite his billion-dollar fortune, he used to put in around 100 hours a week when shooting a film. And he creates hit after hit.

Funnily enough, the way the rich and those who love their jobs feel about work is exactly the reverse of how others look at it. Most people unwillingly drag themselves to work on Monday morning and watch the clock until Friday afternoon when they can finally throw off the shackles they have had to endure for five long and painful days. They only really live for two out of seven days, without taking into consideration that Saturday is generally spent winding down and Sunday is already haunted by the gloomy spectre of Monday-morning blues.

This makes no sense at all to people who love their jobs. A day off, a welcome relief for most people, is almost a form of punishment for the others. One thing is certain:

it's not something they pine for.

The great French mathematician and philosopher Blaise Pascal once said:

The past and present are our means; our one and only future, the end. Thus, we never manage to live, but forever hope to live, and since we are constantly planning on being happy one day, it is inevitable that we never are.

Thomas Watson, one of the creators of the formidable corporation, IBM, continually repeated to his salesmen:

> You'll never be successful if you don't convince yourself that selling is the most interesting thing in the world. Make room in your heart for work and put some heart into your work.

The following confession should prove to you that we were not being facetious when we said that depriving a rich man of his work was to punish him. Soichiro Honda himself even used the word 'punishment'.

> 'When people see me working in the lab, some of them snidely remark that the general has donned his battle fatigued. And yet, God knows that I don't go there with a tragic or military feeling. I go for the simple reason that I love working and it's not because I'm the president that I'm going to deprive myself of this pleasure. Why should a man, on the pretext that he is a company president, spend the entire day twiddling his thumbs behind a desk? Of course there are other ways to occupy yourself.' I don't want to sound condescending, but I do believe that some executives prefer busying themselves with facts and figures or polishing their images instead of coming down to the workshop. The fact is that it would be painful for an engineer like me to devote himself to accounting, especially since I'm lucky enough to have skilled experts in this field working for me. I've always supposed that being a president shouldn't be a punishment.'

Here are a few principles you should reflect on:

- You can do whatever you like, provided you put the necessary energy and determination into it

- There is an ideal job or career waiting just for you. You must start believing it exists
- Having to do unpleasant things to earn a living is a fallacy
- The only way to be happy and make lots of money is to do what you really and truly enjoy doing
- You alone can shape your destiny and do what you enjoy, regardless of obstacles
- The greatest barrier to success is within yourself. What is preventing you from doing what you like is your belief that what is valid for others is not valid for you
- Dare to do what you wish. Get rid of your fear and you shall succeed

Nowadays our thoughts are frequently divorced from our emotions. We try to reason everything out. We deny our feelings and stifle our dreams. We don't believe in putting our hearts into our work. We simply put our heads into it. Unfortunately, most people forget that human being are whole entities. If your heart isn't in what you are doing, success will always elude your grasp. Or if you do grab hold of it, it will soon slip away. We have already mentioned that if you want to achieve your dreams, you must constantly feed them. If your heart is not in your work, find a new job. Or try discovering a new dimension or fresh challenges in your work.

Some people slander successful men and women. They often believe that the rich are crass materialists, cold and calculating, and devoid of all human emotion. What they tend to forget is that all of them are ruled by passion and many by their hearts as well. They are, in fact, 'romantics' in the world of business. They carried their dreams, which were often conceived in childhood, in their hearts and did everything they could to achieve them.

In general, you must start by considering the products or services you have to offer to the public before looking for profits. Money flows in naturally when the product or service is good. Become the best in your field and money will follow. It has been said that anyone who makes the best mouse trap, preaches the best sermon, or writes the best book can build his home in a dense forest; clients will go out of their way to come to him.

DARE TO BE YOURSELF!

People often think that the rich are severe, conformist and attached to traditional values.

But then think again!

Of course being original doesn't mean that they deliberately set themselves apart by concocting some sort of exaggerated character trait or wearing outlandish clothes. What was different was their mentality, as well as the methods they used. They were themselves. Moreover, the fact that they didn't graduate from business schools has perhaps something to do with their originality. School tends to level out the thinking process and to suppress originality, despite its liberal pretensions.

Conformity in thought prevents us from seeing new avenues and different or original solutions. It is possible to doubt the relevance or, in any case, the effectiveness of graduate studies given the track-record achieved by MBAs in business. Furthermore, large firms are increasingly becoming dissatisfied with the rational model of management advocated in the 1960s and are now starting to put more emphasis on on-the-job training. In Japan, business schools simply do not exist. So, how do you account for the 'Japanese miracle' we hear so much about?

Don't misunderstand us. We are not belittling the value of education. Far from it. Technical developments make higher education necessary. Simply put, everything points to the fact that although studying is often necessary, it never seems quite sufficient to guarantee success. Something more is needed - a spark of originality or boldness, which schools fail to teach, indeed, which they often stifle altogether.

Society, schools and education in general all help turn people into clones by eliminating differences and nipping personal aspirations in the bud. This process begins early in life and is often insidious. In fact, people's fears of being different and their need to conform belong to the theory of the subconscious we discussed in Chapter 2.

A tiny inner voice nevertheless survives within each of us. Timid and worried, it whispers to us that our public images are false, that our genuine personalities are hidden and unexpressed. Frustration, sadness, and, in some cases, a feeling of being dead inside are some of the disadvantages we heap upon ourselves.

If you want to succeed, be different from the others. Be yourself. Don't be afraid to assert your true personality. Don't forget that you are unique. As soon as you toe the line, you are denying your true personality.

Repeat the following formulas to yourself:

- Day after day, I'm asserting my true personality more and more
- I'm unique and feel completely free to express my desire to succeed and grow rich
- It's my right and duty to be myself
- The success I achieve will be in keeping with the extent to which I assert myself. I'm asserting myself more and more in all areas of my life
- Every day I'm increasing my self-worth tenfold and becoming more and more successful

One of the richest and undoubtedly the most nonconformist men in the world was Howard Hughes. Naturally his mysterious and eccentric life cannot be used as a role model, but the fact is that he is a spectacular illustration of the principle stating that to succeed you must be true to yourself. The portrait drawn by Max Gunther in his book The Very, Very Rich and How They Got That Way, is quite striking:

He conducted his business from public telephone booths, hotel rooms, wherever he happened to be. Most of the information he needed to run his bewilderingly diverse enterprises — information that the average systematic businessman would store in file cabinets — he stored in his head. His employees and even his close associates seldom knew where he was on any given day. We would dart about among his far-flung ventures with an apparent lack of plan and a total lack of formal scheduling that irritated and confounded the more orderly minded of his executives.

If you wanted to get in touch with him you called a phone number and were plugged into a switchboard that, at various stages of his career, might be in Hollywood, Las Vegas, or Houston. You gave your message to a secretary. A few weeks might go by. Finally, if Hughes felt like talking to you, he would phone you back, perhaps from a neighbouring city, perhaps from halfway around the world. The call might come at 1 a.m. your time. Hughes wouldn't consider that important. It might be 4 a.m. his time.

Gunther then concludes this portrait of the eccentric Howard Hughes, whose life was true to Montaigne's maxim, which says that to succeed you must act like a wise man, but look like a fool:

The formal structures of the business world meant nothing to Hughes: its chain of command, its documents, its timetables. He worked when he wanted to work, sometimes 36 or more hours at a stretch. A fit of work might seize him as readily on a weekend as on a standard business day, as readily after midnight as between 9 a.m. and 5 p.m. 'He was the kind of man', says a Hollywood press agent who knew him in his moviemaking days, 'who broke every rule taught by the Harvard Business School. Every rule except the one that says you should make money.'

The end of this quote contains the key to the behavior of successful nonconformists. They disobeyed all the rules except the one that says you should make money.

Beware of falling into the seemingly harmless trap of conformity. We all naturally tend to imitate everyone else, a tendency we view to be the principle of making the least effort. Unfortunately, the vast majority of people are not successful and lead mediocre lives.

Ray Kroc said,

> I believe that if two of my executives thought the same way, one of them would have to go.

Make sure you never simply follow blindly. Do just the opposite: ensure that your original viewpoint and personal way of thinking render you indispensable.

The richest of men were all individualists and nonconformists. They were not afraid of straying from the beaten track, of hammering out new methods, or of being creative. Aristotle Onassis, the astronomically rich Greek ship owner, was one of those who revelled in nonconformity.

The harvest he reaped was incalculable. His methods were his own personal ones. He often said, many assumed jokingly, that in his office was his little black address book, which he never left behind on transcontinental journeys intended to make his business flourish. No one really knew if he was serious or not, but this book did exist. Onassis' methods resembled those used by Hughes, even though their personalities were very different. Onassis loved the splendour and shine of high society whereas Hughes finished out his life alone, suffering from acute paranoia (a sad ending for such a brilliant mind).

WORKING TO BE THE BEST

The story of Bill Gates' early career and his meteoric rise shows that money, however important a consideration it may be in the eyes of all business people, is not always the be all and end all. In fact, what goads people like him into action is the need to do things well and to accomplish something that will please many people. Because he was not looking for immediate profit, it seems as though the sums he amass are even greater.

Henry Ford was one of those who shared the same philosophy, which is basically a form of humanitarianism and radically changes the image we have of the rich as ruthless exploiters. Several passages in Ford's autobiography reveal this principle. Here is a good example of it:

I determined resolutely that never would I join a company in which finance came before the work or in which bankers or financiers had a part. And further, that if there were no way to get started in the kind of business that I thought could be managed in the interest of the public, then I simply would not get started at all, for my own short experience, together with what 1 saw going on around me, was quite enough proof that business as a mere money-making game was not worth giving much thought to and was distinctly no place for a man who wanted to accomplish anything. Also it did not seem to me to be the way to make money. I have yet to have it demonstrated that it is the way. For the only foundation of real business is service.

Malaysian communications and oil tycoon, T. Ananda Krishnan, unlike many others, never succumbed to the temptation of relating his life story or writing down his success principles. However, he did give a reporter the following advice:

- Take care of your body. Be as good as possible. Don't worry about minor problems. Look at me. I'm no Apollo, but I haven't wasted my time crying about my ethnicity. Remember, you are never taken as seriously by others as you think you are

- Eat moderately; when you have urgent work to do, avoid rich foods and wine. Spending hours at the dinner table, when work is also encroaching on your time, is still the best way of shortening your life

- Wait for the evening to come and don't feast until your cogitations are over. Then have a good meal in the company of your friends and if possible never talk business at the table

- Do the exercise you require and stay fit. Basic yoga is advisable as much for your body as for your mind.
  If you can do judo one or two hours a week, this sport will get rid of all your complexes
  Stay tanned even if you need a sunlamp to do it. For most people, a winter tan means you have just arrived from sunny spots and for everybody, sun means money

- Once you have taken care of your physical appearance, choose a fancy lifestyle. Reside in a beautiful house even if you have to live in the attic; you will frequent rich people in the halls and elevator. Go to elegant cafes even if you have to sip one drink all night long. You will soon learn that solitude haunts those who manage to earn a lot of money

- If you are short of money, borrow some. Never ask for a small amount. Ask for large ones and always pay them back as soon as possible if you can

Never confide your problems in anyone and always pretend you are having a good time

- Don't sleep too much; upon waking up, you might tell yourself that you have failed. Three hours less sleep at night during a year will give you an extra month and a half to succeed.

BECOME AN EXPERT
IN YOUR FIELD

I HAVEN'T A CLUE WHAT I'D LIKE TO DO...

This is unquestionably a common complaint in modern times. Our society seems to be overwhelmed with confusion, a feeling few can escape from. This is largely due to the breakdown in the traditional roles. Times have changed radically, however. Women have joined the workforce and have met with rapid success. As for men, they no longer automatically do what their fathers did. Furthermore, today's career profiles resemble yesterday's very little. People make rapid and often drastic career switches. Choices are no longer as clear as they used to be, both for women, newcomers on the work market, and for men. Alvin Toffler describes this phenomenon well in *Future Shock*, saying that we are now living in a society that offers us an infinite array of choices. Countless new avenues have opened up to people of all ages, traditional roles having gradually lost their hold over us. We are currently living in the transitional period from the Age of Pisces into the Age of the Aquarius. To understand more on this subject, please do your own research on this subject. To put in a nutshell, we are heading into an era where hybrid cars will soon take over gasoline powered cars. Online business will be the eventual mode of transaction. It is here and now.

This choice has led to greater freedom. But it can also mean we no longer know where to turn.

Rapid and profound change is part of the problem of people who can't seem to put their finger on the type of professional activity that would help them get going. But that is not the only thing. The fact that people constantly moan about not knowing what they want to do with their lives is due to their having spent years stifling their aspirations and ignoring their inner selves. By wishing so desperately to conform, they have forgotten who they are, thus sowing their own seeds of confusion.

This uncertainty is all the more serious insofar as anyone who doesn't really know what he wants to do and doesn't establish clear-cut goals for himself will never be able to succeed. The opposite is also true. When you know perfectly well what you want to do in life, when your desire is crystal clear, the conditions enabling you to achieve it soon show up. Often, extremely precise desires come true almost immediately.

And yet, such a thing as a perfectly straightforward desire, that is, devoid of hesitation, ambiguity and contradiction, is very rare indeed. It's not so difficult to find, however. You only need the means to do so. Vague, confused ambitions programme your subconscious to be just as muddled. Since your aspirations are foggy, your results will be likewise. A metamorphosis must take place within yourself — you must get a clear picture of your ambitions and desires. You must shape them, truly sculpt them so that they become blindingly clear and precise.

Don't make the mistake of underestimating the importance of this inner change. Until you are sure what you want, you will not get it.

All the rich had unmistakeable ambitions. Many of them used the expression, 'I knew'. Their career choices were spawned by a deep sense of intuition which left no room for doubt.

> One of the keys to success is knowing
> exactly what you want to do

Many people go through periods of hesitation and uncertainty. They are at a dead end, not knowing how to overcome this state of confusion. The most important thing to do is to actively decide to change this character trait.

It can easily be done. Many have done so already. Self-suggestion is the road to this transformation.

Relax and withdraw into yourself. Drop your guard and usual barriers. Let your thoughts and imagination flow freely. Recall the old dreams you abandoned along the way; they often contain the seeds of your true vocation in life.

Submit your dream to your subconscious and repeat formulas such as:

- My subconscious will infallibly help me discover how I can be a complete success in life and make all the money I need
- I'm worthy of a job that pleases me 100 per cent and allows me to grow rich beyond all my wildest dreams
- I'm successful
- My life is a triumph
- I do what truly pleases me, so I excel in my job and my income is constantly increasing
- I'm unique. My self-worth is growing every day and allows me to do a job that I like and that pays me well.

Issue the following command to your subconscious:

Subconscious, help me discover what I really like

Fall asleep knowing perfectly well that the answer already lies within you and that you have already obtained what you asked for. The formidable power of your subconscious will work continuously for you day and night, as long as you have steered it in the right direction.

Besides making use of these powerful techniques, you can also consult specialists in career counselling, your friends, newspapers, and magazines. Each decade has its own particular trends. Nowadays, computers are the state of the art. The author of the bestseller Megatrends states that since 1985, 75 per cent of all jobs are linked directly or indirectly to computers and computer science. This trend will surely not disappear any time soon. By the year 2000, all jobs will probably be affected by computers. We have seen it. This could be a clue for you. Even if computers don't interest you as such, they will probably be useful to you.

Needless to say, our intention is not to push you into one field rather than another. This would be a foolish thing to do, since it's not enough for something to be fashionable for you to be interested in it. Instead of blindly following trends, stick to your inner feelings. Keep a close watch on whatever is currently popular, but place more importance on your personal inclinations.

DO FOR YOURSELF WHAT YOU ALREADY DO FOR OTHERS

One of the most profitable things you could do is to set up your own business in a field you have already worked in. Experience has shown that this is one of the surest avenues to success because you probably already know this field well. In fact, one of the fundamentals of success is having an in-depth knowledge, also called a 'specialization' of the area you are about to embark in. A lack of knowledge is one of the major causes of failure. Both these points shall be examined in detail in the rest of this chapter.

THE SECRET OF A TRUE EDUCATION

Earlier on we spoke about education and its role in success. Several of the richest men whose lives we have analysed did not go to university. The same goes for countless other millionaires, and this has led many analysts to wonder whether education actually hinders success. We, however, wouldn't go that far. Besides, all it would take to refute this argument would be to cite the case of Paul Getty, who graduated from Oxford University.

Formal education is not detrimental in itself, especially in our society, where science and technology have become so advanced. However, several people, including millionaires, have mentioned that there could be certain disadvantages, one being the length of study courses, which inevitably delay going out into the world to make millions. Many long and perhaps important years are lost in this way. Those setting out to become rich at the ages of 18 or 20 are generally five or six years ahead of university graduates.

In his book *The Very, Very Rich,* Max Gunther comments on how remarkable it is that so few fabulously wealthy men even bothered to finish college or even school for that matter and includes some of their academic records to illustrate his point. For example, Clement Stone dropped out of high school believing that it had nothing to do with the goal he had set for himself. Howard Hughes "had money and leisure to attend college but refused." William Lear was a "school dropout."

During the Second World War, Henry Ford was treated as an ignorant pacifist by a *Chicago Tribune* reporter. Ford, insulted by this slanderous remarks, decided to sue, charging the newspaper with libel. This is how Napoleon Hill relates this enlightening story in his book *Grow Rich With peace of Mind:*

When the attorneys for the *Tribune* had Mr Ford on the witness stand they cross-examined him in an attempt to prove their statement was true. One question they asked him was: "How many soldiers did the British send over to subdue the rebellion in the colonies in 1776?" With a grin, Ford replied: "I don't know just how many, but I have heard it was a lot more than ever went back." There was laughter from the court, the jury, the spectators, and even from the frustrated lawyer who had asked the question. Ford kept calm through an hour or more of similar questioning on "schoolbook" topics. At length, in reply to a question which was particularly obnoxious to him, the industrialist let off some steam. He observed that he had a row of electric push-buttons hanging over his desk, and that when he wanted a question answered, he placed his finger on the right button and called in the eight man to answer that question. He wanted to know why he should burden his mind with a lot of useless details when he had able men around him who could supply him with all the information he needed.

Long-term studies are also liable to dampen a person's boldness, sense of initiative, or risk-taking ability, since logical reasoning and analysis are often given priority over action.

In his book *The Rich and Super Rich*, Ferdinand Lundberg states the following:

> Educators, trying in desperation to rally popular support for education, and mulling over statistics, like to point out to philistines that on average educated people earn more than the meagerly educated. And this is true when it comes to offering marketable skills for modest salaries in an existing establishment that requires ever-increasing skilled personnel for its complex operations. But it has never been true where

really big money is concerned. An education can be a severe handicap when it comes to making money.

He goes on to say:

The reason for this is that in the process of being educated there is always the danger that the individual will acquire scruples, a fact dimly sensed by some of the neo-conservatives who rail against the school system as "communistic". These scruples, unless they are (diluted), are a distinct handicap to the fully fledged money-maker, who must in every situation be opportunistic. But a person who has had it deeply impressed upon him that he must make *exact* reports of *careful* laboratory experiments, must produce *exact* translations and echoes of foreign languages, must write *faithful* reports of *correct* readings and must be at least imaginatively aware of the world in its diversity, and who has learned these lessons well, must invariably discover that some element of scrupulousness – even if he hasn't been subject to moral indoctrination – has been impressed on his psyche. If he enters upon money-making in a world bazaar where approximate truths, vague deceptions, sneak manoeuvres, half promises and even bald falsehoods are the widely admired and heavily regarded order of the day he must [adjust] his standards. The very process of laboriously making the adjustment, even if he succeeds, puts him at a disadvantage *vis-a-vis* the unschooled, who need waste no energy on such adjustments, who pick up anything lying around loose as easily as they breathe.

We must nonetheless admit that education does contain positive elements. In our society, a diploma opens up many doors. Of course, this does not necessarily guarantee you success, but often gives you your first opportunity. General knowledge can also be valuable.

Since success is always linked to other people and nobody ever gets rich completely on his own, some knowledge of psychology, sociology, and history, to name a few fields, allows us to broaden our vision and fine-tune our judgement. This knowledge is, of course, valid only if you know how to put it to good use.

The most important point concerning the relationship between education and success is this: even if many of the rich did not attend school for very long, all of them, without exception, became experts in their fields.

All of them made sure that they learned as much as possible about their areas of business. Refusing to bend to this necessity inevitably leads to failure and condemns us to mediocrity.

The spectacular rise of computers, along with the growing numbers of researchers in all domains, has caused a rapid evolution in the facts we assume to be true. We live in a world that is in a perpetual state of motion but which is relatively constant at the same time. Those who long for success must keep learning more and more about their fields throughout their lives. What you discover today could very well be obsolete tomorrow. To keep up to date with the rapid evolution of society, you must stay on your toes and live in a state of wonder and curiosity to sustain your desire to learn.

Knowing as much as possible about your discipline and becoming the best in it are absolute musts. This is the educational style of the rich. Besides, unlike some academically-trained entrepreneurs, others on the road to success are not afraid to roll up their sleeves and get their hands dirty.

In many cases, their desire to know everything in their speciality areas appeared excessive, even a manic obsession. Yet, their determination to do things carefully and to take note of the tiniest details was most often responsible for their success.

Ray Kroc became almost lyrical when he spoke about the hamburger bun, confirming the principle we have just stated:

> Consider, for example, the hamburger bun. It requires a certain kind of mind to see beauty in a hamburger bun. Yet, is it any more unusual to find grace in the texture and softly curved silhouette of a bun than to reflect lovingly on the hackles of a favourite fishing fly? Or the arrangement of the textures and colours in a butterfly's wings? Not if you are a McDonald's man. Not if you view the bun as an essential material in the art of serving a great many meals fast. Then this plump yeasty mass becomes an object worthy of sober study.

The way Kroc talks about French fries is no less surprising, at least for those in the know. His search to discover the marvellous taste of the McDonald brothers' fries before he had bought the company was like, the tireless work of a detective hunting for clues in a murder mystery novel. Later on he continued to perfect them until he had them just right. His efforts produced results since one part of McDonalds' popularity is due to the taste of its French fries.

Spielberg is also a movie 'maniac' in the sense that he gets involved in every aspect of production: the screen play, of course, but also casting, music, editing and special effects. He leaves nothing to chance and watches over each production stage.

Honda, never hesitated to throw on overalls and lend a hand in the workshop either, even after he had become a company president. A simple-hearted man despite his prestige, he never stopped wanting to learn.

THE MAGIC OF GOALS

Once you have discovered the field in which you wish to excel and grow rich – and you now have the means to do so – you can concentrate on carrying out your plan. You will realize by now that some of the best plans are actually quite simple. Every large company started out small, and was generally the brainchild of one individual alone whose values, enthusiasm, and dreams took concrete shape. Let us hear what Thomas Peters and Robert Waterman have to say about the paradox of simplicity in *In Search of Excellence* :

We will conclude with one strange contradiction that may really hold. We call it the smart-dumb rule. Many of today's managers – MBA-trained and the like – may be a little bit too smart for their own good. The smart ones are the ones who shift direction all the time, based upon the latest output from the expected value equation. The ones who juggle hundred-variable models with facility; the ones who design complicated incentive systems; the ones who wire up matrix structures; the ones who have 200-page strategic plans and 500-page market requirement documents that are but step one in product development exercises.

Our 'dumber' friends are different. They just don't understand why every customer can't have personalized service, even in the potato chip business. They are personally affronted … when a bottle of beer goes sour. They can't understand why a regular flow of new products isn't possible, or why a worker can't contribute a suggestion every couple of weeks. Simple-minded fellows, really; simplistic even. Yes, simplistic has a negative connotation. But the people who lead the excellent companies are a bit simplistic.

> You must set yourself a precise target,
> an amount and a deadline to make it

Some of you are probably beginning to wonder why we are wasting your time. Yet, what has probably kept you form succeeding up to now is the fact that you have not obeyed this rule, or that you haven't set yourself a goal because you limited yourself subconsciously.

Remember, people who fail never have precise goals. Or perhaps, at a more secret and subtle level and for all sorts of subconscious reasons, they set themselves unrealistically low objectives. In other words, they succeed in being failures.

This reminds us of a story often told in books. It's the one about an insurance salesman who could never sell more than €5,000 worth of premiums a month. When assigned to a territory where sales were well below this amount, he always managed to reach this €5,000 target. However, when he was sent to a larger territory where other salesmen were performing much better than this, he was never able to top his €5,000 average. The dilemma facing him was clearly based on goals and self-image (we will discuss their close interrelationship shortly). He didn't believe that he could sell more (or less) than €5,000 and his subconscious target was set accordingly. This is proof of the power of the subconscious and the fact that it can be either easy or difficult for our subconscious to help us reach any objective.

Consider your own experiences. Haven't they always been directly linked to your objective? Anyone with a vague, uncertain target or none at all will get results that match this. On the other hand, anyone who has a specific goal and puts a specific plan of action into motion always achieves it.

Why is this? The theory of the subconscious provides the solution. A target is the most simple and effective way of programming your subconscious. It's a kind of secret password, and it is indispensable in gaining access to the world of success. You won't necessarily have to work harder to achieve this goal and you might even have to work less, especially if you are among those who feel that they don't reap the benefits of their efforts.

Don't get us wrong. You normally have to work very hard to succeed. But it is possible to work less and get better results. You can work the same number of hours as usual and increase your results. Once again, the secret lies in your goal.

One thing is sure, even among those who are hard-working and have success-orientated qualities: most people do not have a specific objective in mind. Most people are satisfied with a slight improvement in their lives without ever considering or daring to set themselves a clear-cut figure.

What about you? What is your goal for next year? How much do you want to earn? €20,000? €30,000? €50,000? €100,000? Half a million? A million?

If you are already earning a salary, you know that your career is following its normal course, and that if you do nothing special to change it, you will be entitled to a preset raise, generally a meager one. If this satisfies you, so much the better. But if you want your lifestyle to improve substantially – a perfectly legitimate desire – ask your-self what goal you have set for yourself. Many salaried workers, who complain about the pittance they make, state that their situations are hopeless and that even if they established a goal for themselves, they wouldn't have time to find the means to achieve it. This is simply an excuse.

If your job promises no foreseeable raise or promotion, and thwarts your objective, make sure that as soon as you leave work, and despite your family obligations, you spend at least an hour or two searching for new opportunities. It's the only way to get out of your current situation, and it's not as hard as it sounds. If, on the other hand, you ease up at the end of your work day and indulge only in leisure activities, it is most unlikely, impossible even, that you will ever better your situation.

If you want a brighter future for yourself, discover your goals and work out how much time and energy you are willing to channel into reaching them. If all you can do is dream of getting a promotion or a fantastic job offer, but haven't fixed a specific objective, the 'miracle' you are expecting will never happen. Your self-worth is exactly what you think it is.

Let's start with a simple little test. Take a piece of paper and write down how much you'd like to earn next year. Finished? Good. Now read what follows very carefully.

> When you created your goal, you automatically based it on your self-image

If your current salary is €12,000 a year, you perhaps started to write down that you would like to earn €25,000.

But you immediately stopped yourself and put £20,000 instead or, if you were feeling optimistic, £22,000. The reason you subconsciously checked yourself was because you believe you are not really worth £25,000 a year, and that you have neither the qualities nor the potential to qualify you for such a generous reward, or perhaps, that your circumstances would never in a million years enable you to reach such a salary. In other words, although this might surprise you, you are worth exactly what you think you are worth. But the reasons you mentally conjured up to limit or reduce your objective appeared reasonable and logical. They are neither. They are purely and simply the products of your self-image.

AIM HIGH!

Remember the important principle we indicated earlier. The greatest limitations people can impose on themselves are the ones created in their own minds. We have established that a person's worth is what he believes it to be. As a rule, most people underestimate themselves, even if they appear self-confident. Those who think deep down that they are truly valuable are few and far between. Everyone has an inferiority complex to some degree, and it causes them to believe that they are not worthy of success, of other people's esteem or of much money.

The best way to increase your worth is to build up yourself-esteem. We have already seen the techniques you could use to bring about this fundamental change. One of the best ways of accomplishing this is to work with a monetary objective.

Do the following exercise. A few moments ago, you set yourself a goal. Double it right away. Now, assess your reaction. Let's say you wrote down £25,000 a year. Why didn't you put £50,000? How do you feel about this target? Do you think it's completely far- etched? Do you think that £50,000 is a lot? You're right in a way, since only a small percentage of people can hope for such an income. And yet, each year, thousands of people around the world become millionaires. And thousands of people have yearly incomes far in excess of £100,000.

All rich people, men and women alike, started out with the self-image of a millionaire before becoming one. To increase your self-worth, aim high. Don't be afraid of doing so. For the first year, however, don't set yourself an amount that will appear totally unrealistic to you. Do it step by step, but make it ambitious enough. If you aim high and almost make it, you will still have achieved a satisfying result. But if your target is low and you barely make it, you will be disappointed and will have made very little progress.

Setting yourself an exact objective is truly magical. What usually happens the first time you set yourself a monetary goal is that you keep a measure of scepticism that limits your ambitions. But as soon as you achieve your first goal, you can and must set yourself even higher goals. And what generally surprises those who set themselves a target for the first time is that they reach it! Not only this, they often go beyond it. Why don't you do the same? Challenge yourself to reach your goal. It's an exciting game that normally brings surprising dividends. Perhaps you will reach your goal in six months instead of the year you had initially given yourself. You will be the first to benefit from this.

You are worth much more than you believe

You are worth infinitely more than you believe. The only problem is that no one has ever told you this before. People have probably done their utmost to persuade you that the opposite is true. Keep this point well in mind: intelligence, work, motivation, imagination, discipline, and experience are of course important ingredients for success, but how many people do you know who have these qualities and who still do not succeed at all or live up to their full potential? Perhaps the same is true for you. Despite your obvious talents and efforts, success seems to inexplicably escape you. Conversely, you have met people at work or in rival firms who do not appear to be gifted with special qualities - and who are not, in fact — but they get the raise in salary that you deserve or present a year-end balance-sheet that makes their associates or stockholders swell with pride.

The real reason is not due to luck or coincidence. These people have different self-images and have set themselves precise goals. They sincerely believe that they deserve substantial incomes. They harbour no doubts about this at all. As for you, it is probable that deep down, without knowing it, you do not believe that you deserve a high income.

Get rid of your mental limitations and increase your self-worth by aiming as high as possible. And remember that it is no harder for your subconscious to help you reach a higher objective than a lower one. And one thing is sure, it will be so much more enjoyable, for this is the start of your journey towards success!

WRITE YOUR GOAL DOWN

...the discipline of writing something down is the first step towards making it happen. In conversation, you can get away with all kinds of vagueness and nonsense, often without even realizing it. But there's something about putting your thoughts on paper that forces you to get down to specifics. That way, it's harder to deceive yourself — or anybody else.

These sharp-minded and psychologically astute words were written by Lee Iacocca.

Take the time to re-read this quote, written by a man who, over the years, displayed the exceptional qualities of a leader of men and of a creator.

'The discipline of writing something down is the first step toward making it happen.' This is by no means a trivial statement. It is very meaningful. The act of writing down your goal makes it concrete. Writing it down is equivalent to going ahead with your first action; it is the first step towards achieving it. And since you must take the first step, you can imagine how important this action is.

The second advantage of Iacocca's method is that you can no longer deceive yourself. Don't be afraid to announce your objective, or at least open up about it to your family and close friends. Naturally, you're running the risk of being the butt of jokes and of sarcasm. But rest assured: all successful people have had to put up with this too. They would never laugh at you. They might smile a bit, but theirs is the smile of an ally who understands that you too have found the secret and will soon be joining them in the circle of winners. As for the rest, ignore their mockery and snide remarks. Soon it will be your turn to laugh. You know a truth that they are unaware of and do not wish to share:

> **A precise goal is the springboard for any accomplishment**

A MAGNIFICENT OBSESSION

Make your goal your magnificent obsession. Write it down in several places. Keep it well in sight. Above all, keep it constantly in mind. A major principle ruling the mind is that energy goes wherever your thoughts go. By constantly thinking of your goal and making it become a fixed idea, all your energy will channel itself into helping you be successful. Better still, thanks to the mysterious work of your subconscious, circumstances and people will help you reach your goal in a new and surprising way. A goal is like magnifying glass. It focuses your energy on your target.

This fixed idea, called 'monoideism' by some writers, not only allows you to increase your energy and success coefficient but prevents a very serious mistake — that of scattering your energy. All rich people had a fixed idea and this goal led them to success.

Another advantage of singlemindedness is that it enables you to direct your professional and overall life more precisely. How does it do this? Very simply. Everything that helps you come closer to your goal must be encouraged. Everything that distances you from it must be rejected. How can you know if something brings you nearer to or farther from your goal? A well-programmed subconscious will tell you in its usual way. You will have a feeling of intuition or you will be influenced by a book you might have read, or by a friend's or a partner's advice.

**To succeed, work hard, never give up,
and above all cherish a magnificent obsession**

Regardless of origin, wealth seemed accessible to anyone willing to put in the effort and take charge of his destiny.

A PLAN OF ACTION

What is surprising when we set a goal for ourselves that is the least bit ambitious is that it normally creates a sudden, compelling insight for us. This realization is usually something like this:

> It is obvious that I won't earn £5,000, £10,000, or £100,000 more this year, or land a new job, or get a promotion if I do nothing about it. If things stay the way they are, I'm going to find myself in basically the same position at the end of the year as I'm in now. I must therefore do something about this. I need a plan of action to reach my goal.

This reasoning is right. Often, you must do something totally different. It's good to become aware of this. Some jobs will unfortunately never make you rich. For example, no civil servant has ever become a millionaire. Some senior government officials are relatively well paid, but they are the exceptions. This is just one example among many. A grocery clerk or a shoe salesperson can become a millionaire — there are many examples of this — but certainly not in this minimum-wage type of job. So, if you are burning with ambition, choose to work in a field full of potential. May we remind you that you must come to grips with the fact that your financial condition will not improve if you do nothing about it.

DEVELOPING YOUR PLAN OF ACTION

If you are looking for your first job, type up your curriculum vitae, make telephone calls, and line up some interviews. If you are looking for a good opportunity in which to invest some money — for example, in real estate — stay on the look-out. Talk to people you know who work in this field, read specialist magazines, go hunting for opportunities. If you want a raise, analyse your situation well. Find the person in the best position to help you get it. Try to formulate the best arguments to describe to your boss how he will benefit from giving you a raise. If you are an entrepreneur, do your best to discover new markets, to capitalize on current markets, or to reduce your costs.

We are aware that these suggestions are over-generalized. This is inevitable. Each situation is special and we don't have the space here to describe how to write up a CV, shine in an interview, or find out about the profitability of a real estate deal. We recommend that you do some serious reading on these topics, especially if you are inexperienced in these areas.

The most vital step is to prepare a step by step plan of action so that your intentions become possible. You must also stick to your original plan, despite the problems and obstacles that may arise. However, it is also essential to know how to make adjustments when necessary and to adopt a better plan when one comes to mind. You must also be able to ditch a plan when failure is looming on the horizon. Some products never catch the public's eye or become popular. Certain jobs in some companies will never be within your reach. But console yourself with the idea that you might find a better one elsewhere. This will happen if your subconscious is programmed positively.

No human being is infallible, not even the most experienced businessperson. Only those who do nothing never make mistakes. The law of averages, which we mentioned previously, as well as a positive mental attitude, will come to your rescue. What counts is that, even if you undergo temporary setbacks, you will still achieve your goals, if your subconscious is properly programmed.

The only difference is that it will take a slightly different and sometimes unexpected path. This is the secret power of a precise monetary goal and a deadline. All roads lead to Rome, so the saying goes. The subconscious seems to have appropriated this adage. These roads are sometimes mysterious, but one thing definitely isn't — your goal.

When making up your plan, be both rigid and flexible, remembering that too much of either one or other can cause you problems. But remember this as well: most people fail because they give up too quickly after their first failure or setback. So, if you are faced with a choice to make, stick to your original plan. All the rich and successful did precisely this.

To apply your plan of action, you will probably be forced to take certain risks, which are sure to make you feel insecure, especially if it's the first time you have set a goal for yourself and hammered out a plan of action. Any change generates a measure of anxiety and insecurity. Don't be afraid to forge ahead. In his memoirs, Lee Iacocca commented on this:

> A certain amount of risk-taking is essential. I realize it's not for everybody. There are some people who won't leave home in the morning without an umbrella, even if the sun is shining. Unfortunately, the world doesn't always wait for you while you try to anticipate your losses. Sometimes you just have to take a chance — and correct your mistakes as you go along.

If you count yourself among those who never leave home without an umbrella, even when the sun is shining, it is highly unlikely that you will have seen fit to set yourself a new objective and establish a plan of action to reach it.

A goal doesn't involve only money. You could set your sights on becoming the best lawyer, the best novelist, the best accountant, the best real estate investor, the best insurance broker or the best shoe manufacturer within a given period of time. This is perfectly legitimate. Besides, it's one of the best ways to achieve success. Remember the true definition of wealth: it is the reward you receive in exchange for services you have rendered to people. If you give the best service, then you can expect your reward to be in keeping with that. The same rules apply for any other kind of goal. In fact, ideally, it's best to combine the two: the desire to become the best in a given field and to receive a specific income within a set time. This combination is particularly effective.

NO MORE THAN TWO GOALS AT A TIME

Be careful not to set yourself too many goals at the same time. This rarely, if ever, leads to success. However, wishing to become the best in your field and to make a specific
income does not constitute two goals, it is a double aim, since both desires are intimately linked.

WHAT DO YOU WANT TO DO WITH YOUR LIFE?

Limiting yourself to two objectives a year such as becoming an expert in your field, reaching a set income, or getting a new job, doesn't mean that you shouldn't set yourself long-term goals. It wouldn't be a bad idea to establish a five-year goal that would naturally overlap with your one-year goal. Many rich people go so far as to set goals for their whole lives. You might well have noticed that several of the men we have met up with knew what they wanted to do with their lives even when they were very young. The expression 'I knew that my whole life would be devoted to such and such an activity,' is a common one.

Why not follow their example? Put your book down for a minute and ask yourself what you want to do with your life, what you want to be. Don't limit yourself. Let your imagination run riot. You are alone. No one is there to criticize you or to sneer at you. What kind of person would you like to be in 5, 10, or 25 years from now? What kind of life are you dreaming of? What job would you like to have? Disregard your present situation, previous failures, and past life. Forget about your age, as well. Remember Ray Kroc, who believed at the age of 52 that the best was yet to come. You can make your life rich and full at any age. And often the dreams you nourish come true much more easily than you realize, and come true regardless of your age or current situation.

The advantage of knowing what you would like to do for the rest of your life and to picture yourself in the distant future is that it gives meaning to your short-term goals. Take a piece of paper and write down what you would like to do with your life. Add as many details as possible. What kind of work would you like to be doing? How much money would you like to be earning? In 5 years? In 10 years? In 25 years from now? What kind of house would you like to live in? What kind of friends would you like to have? Will travelling be part of your life? What about vacations? Your family life?

Write all of this down in as much detail as possible. Picturing your life in this way can literally shape your future. In fact, by dreaming like this you are programming your subconscious. You are flooding it with images that are likely to come true in your life. The advantage is that you hold the reins of command. You become the architect of your own life.

As of now, you can become the architect of your life

This long-term objective will become your ideal in life and will simplify many of the choices facing you which would otherwise have been difficult to make, or worse still, would have appeared arbitrary, or even absurd, to you. When you don't know what you want to do with your life, it is difficult to justify the most insignificant day-to-day decisions. They don't seem to be part of a greater plan that gives meaning to your actions and even thoughts. Those who don't know what they want in life or can't picture their future, cannot shape it to suit their desires and rarely, if ever, achieve success. They are like rudderless ships floating on the sea.

Making up a life plan is very stimulating and motivating, and it contributes to success in all areas of life. However, always keep in mind the need to remain flexible regarding the future, since life involves constant adaptation. What you will be doing in five or ten years from now won't necessarily be what you had expected. This doesn't mean that whatever happens to you can't be even better than you had dreamed possible. When our minds are well programmed, the situations which develop are always better. As you develop your potential and become more and more positive, the plans you dream up will be bolder, more ambitious, and you will, most likely, drop some of your initial ones. Don't worry. This is what often happens in life. What counts is your constant progression towards greater self-fulfillment and total personal enrichment.

IDENTIFY NEXT YEAR'S OBJECTIVE

Once you have your goal clearly in mind for the year to come, divide it up. Put in order the things you must accomplish. Don't forget to write all of this down. Set a date for each of the stages, and respect your new deadlines. Try to see whether your monthly income equals a twelfth of the amount you intend to earn as outlined in your new goal. If you get paid on a regular basis and there's no way you will be earning a twelfth of your goal in one month, you must clearly do something else. This does not necessarily mean quitting your job, but it may mean doing something extra to reach your objective.

Of course, some incomes can't be divided in such a clear-cut way. But there is certainly one thing that you can and must plan out as carefully as possible, while still remaining flexible enough to respond if a once-in-a-lifetime opportunity arises, and that is the work and effort you must put in to reach your goal. Divide your yearly goal into months, and then into weeks. Sound planning prevents a lot of worry.

DISCIPLINE YOURSELF!

It's all well and good to set yourself an objective, and it is necessary for anyone wishing to grow rich, but to try to work towards it day by day, you need discipline. And the best discipline is the one that you, and no one else, impose on yourself. The Greek philosopher, Heraclitus, said: 'Character equals destiny.' Think about this simple, but profound, equation. Look at the people around you. Think of those you know. There are no exceptions to this rule. All successful men and women have strong characters and temperaments: they are highly disciplined. Consider the people you know. You will see that no one succeeds without strength of character. Everyone has a master. To become your own master and take your destiny in hand, you need discipline. Incidentally, all the rich men quoted in this book were all rigidly disciplined. This disproves the popular notion that the rich are idle and lazy. True, some inheritors are the proverbial idle rich, but this because they simply didn't need strength of character and self-discipline to earn their money; it was handed to them on a silver platter. The opposite is true for the self-made men of today.

Character equals destiny

You mustn't believe that when we say discipline we mean behaviour that leaves no room for fantasy and relaxation. Disciplining yourself also means putting time aside for leisure activities, relaxation and physical exercise. The mistake many people who are setting out to build a fortune make is to lose sight of the fact that they need to take breaks to function well. Overworking is never productive. You have to devote time to recharging your batteries. You need to find an equilibrium.

Many people are overworked but never accomplish much. Complaining of overwork is fashionable these days. And yet, the vast majority of people don't use a tenth of their potential.

Those who manage to work so hard are not really different from the rest of us. They are not more energetic, either. However, they do know how to use their energy better. Whereas it lies dormant in most people, they have awakened it. You now know how to do it, too. Furthermore, these highly disciplined men and women have developed sound working habits. For most people, the problem is that they have picked up bad habits. Through discipline and positive mental programming, you will be able to develop the habit of success.

Success is a habit

Become a slave to the habits of success in the same way as you have, until now, been the slave to habits leading you to failure. By replacing one with the other, you will create a new habit, and a new second nature to yourself. Success will then be irresistibly attracted to you. Cultivate the habit of success and self-discipline every hour and every day of your life.

LEARNING TO WORK EFFECTIVELY

HOW TO MAKE EACH YEAR HAVE 13 MONTHS

If you are not used to working hard, start little by little. Gradually increase your rhythm. At the beginning, try working one hour extra each day. By the end of the week, you will have put five extra hours towards success. By the end of the year, you will have contributed 250 additional hours to success. A normal work week contains 40 hours. These 250 extra hours will have earned you 6 extra weeks. Your new year will comprise 58 weeks instead of 52. As such, you will have worked more than 13 months that year. This could give you a considerable edge over your colleagues. Now picture working two extra hours a day. You will have made 500 extra hours in a single year, yet all these added hours will not make you any more tired. It's simply a matter of habit.

SUCCESS MUST BECOME YOUR ONLY HABIT!

Stay alert to your success habits. Never hesitate to put yourself into question on a regular basis and to review your plan of action. This is one of the keys to success.

Always try to improve your skills and aptitudes. Never believe that you are infallible. Reconsider your methods. Perfect them constantly!:

FINISH IN ONE HOUR WHAT YOU USUALLY DO IN THREE

Working one or two extra hours a day is a constructive thing to do, but more profitable still is increasing your effectiveness by finishing in one hour what you normally take several to do. The secrets of enhancing your efficiency are these: first, you must establish different deadlines, meaning shorter ones, and secondly, you must improve your concentration.

Let's start with the first point. Scientific studies carried out by psychologists have shown that the time needed to accomplish a task can be reduced considerably (up to a reasonable limit) without the quality of the work being sacrificed. It has even been proven that in some cases the quality has actually risen. Furthermore, some people can not function without very short deadlines.

Studies conducted on a large number of subjects demonstrate the following rule: *The average individual tends to need all the time he is allowed to do a certain task even when he could finish the same task more quickly if an emergency arose.*

Reducing the time needed to do a task is once again related to the subconscious. What people do when they set themselves or are given a deadline is to programme their subconscious. We have already seen that it is not any more difficult for the subconscious to programme itself for failure than for success, since it is a power that is blind, so to speak, or neutral at least. Similarly, it is not any harder for your subconscious to help you accomplish a task in less time, so long as it is actually feasible, of course. The subconscious is much more powerful than you believe it to be — and faster. In fact, it can provide you with an endless amount of creative energy.

Being aware of the two laws regarding time and productivity can have dramatic practical consequences. The time needed to do a job is much more flexible than people generally believe. So, if you want to do in an hour what you usually do in three, pretend you only have an hour in which to do it in.

In other words, invent an urgency. In so doing, you are issuing an order to your subconscious. Try it. The results will surprise you. This doesn't mean to say that you have to activate yourself with black coffee as the French writer, Balzac, used to do. He, incidentally, provides us with an astonishing example of how well you can work when you have a strict deadline. In order to put himself under pressure, and in a state of peak creativity, he would promise to submit his manuscripts to his editors in what seemed like unrealistically short periods of time. It was in this way that he managed to write 300-page masterpieces in two weeks. Of course, this great writer had his share of talent and skill, but never make the mistake of underestimateing yourself. You have probably been doing so for much too long already. You, too, are talented. You, too, can work fast and well... and without causing yourself extra stress. You can do it as soon as you believe you can. . . and as soon as you try it.

Set yourself tighter deadlines; you will accomplish more without sacrificing quality

Let's consider the second point now: concentration. It is one of the fundamental keys to success in every single field. Closely related to this is the fact that anyone who cannot concentrate seriously on what he is doing will never be able to succeed. It is absolutely impossible. All rich people are and were superb concentrators. Howard Hughes left the impression that he was simply an extravagant millionaire, an impression confirmed by those who knew him intimately. But those people overlooked his exceptional ability to concentrate. In his book *The Very, Very Rich*, Max Gunther writes:

> Hughes worked on his film personally, constantly changing hats as he flitted from scriptwriting to directing to set designing to editing. He often worked more than 24 hours at a stretch without even pausing for a nap. 'I never, saw a man who could concentrate that hard or for that long,'

said Jean Harlow, who seemed to be [attracted to] Hughes but who never received [any attention] in return.

Honda was also a remarkable example of deep concentration. When he was a novice inventor, so he recounts, he was always completely absorbed in his work. No one could have broken his concentration, not even his closest friends with whom he loved to go out and have fun. At dinnertime, his mother would call the family to come in and eat, but his mind was elsewhere.

Paul Getty was also so wrapped up in his work during the early stages of his career that he would often stay up all night.

The author of *The Practice of Meditation* recounts the following anecdote:

> One day a man of note invited Isaac Newton to dinner. Newton arrived and sat down in the living room. But his host, who had forgotten about his guest, ate his dinner and went back to his business affairs. Meanwhile, Newton, completely engrossed in important scientific matters, didn't budge an inch. He forgot about the dinner and sat on the sofa as motionless as a statue. The next morning, his host spotted him still sitting there in his living room and remembered his invitation. He was naturally upset by his faux-pas and apologized profusely.

All these stories are fine, you say, but the truth of the matter is, you simply can't concentrate. You complain about this regularly since you are aware that it does you a lot of harm. Don't worry. There are a number of easy exercises that can help you to increase your concentration. The first one is to repeat, preferably at night, during your daily self-suggestion session, the following formula, or any other that you might have adopted.

> **My concentration is getting better every day. I can now do all of my tasks more quickly and efficiently**

The second exercise is extremely powerful and has been used for centuries. It can produce miracles in your life, and will increase your powers of concentration.

CONCENTRATION EXERCISE

Draw a black dot about a quarter of an inch in diameter on a cardboard sheet and stick it to the wall or put it on the floor in front of you. Sit down comfortably, breathing slowly, and stare at this dot, trying not to blink. After a while, your eyes will begin to itch. Close your eyes and open them again. Start over. Don't worry, this exercise will not harm your eyes. On the contrary, it strengthens the optical nerve and can even help some eye disorders.

Start by spending two or three minutes on this exercise, gradually increasing the time. By the end of the first week, you should have reached five minutes. When you have reached approximately 20 minutes, your concentration will be excellent. To occupy your thoughts during this exercise and to maximize its effects, why not repeat some of your favourite auto-suggestion formulas?

You will discover a noticeable improvement in your powers of concentration even by the first day if you have spent a few minutes on it. The results will speak for themselves. You will be able to concentrate longer and better. Problems that appear complex to you will seem simple. Your thoughts will speed up. You will easily do in one hour what you normally did in three. And you will do it better, more precisely and neatly. This exercise also enhances your memory, the source of all logical reasoning. Another consequence is more acute presence of mind. This, in fact, is normal, since when you are concentrating you are sharply aware of the moment passing and of the situation in hand. The right answer, the one that always used to come to you too late, will appear more naturally at the right moment. You will be better able to seize opportunities instead of letting them slip by.

In addition, this exercise also helps develop your sense of intuition. This is especially useful in business. Some people will claim that they don't have 20 minutes to spend on this exercise each day. (Daily practice is, in fact, recommended, especially every morning shortly after waking up to 'warm up' the 'muscles' of your mind.) The busier you are during the day, the more you will feel the need to do this exercise. To a certain extent, it is when you don't have 'a minute to yourself' that it becomes imperative for you to take a few minutes out to do this concentration exercise. As soon as you can see the results of this exercise, it will become part of your daily routine.

You probably know that the amount of concentration you put into an activity is directly proportional to the pleasure you get out of it. Take an interesting book or movie, for example, or even a love affair. In all of these situations, your level of concentration is very high; you are so engrossed in it that you sometimes feel hypnotized. What is the reason for this? These activities please you, fascinate you. If concentration is the, key to success and our level of concentration relies on the pleasure we get from an activity, then in order to succeed, we must do what we enjoy. We have again reached the same conclusion we discussed earlier, but this time a different logic has led us there.

ONCE YOU HAVE SET YOURSELF A GOAL, KEEP AT IT UNTIL YOU SUCCEED

You must cultivate persistence and the habit of believing that every failure is just a temporary setback. Failure is a step that will lead you to success, provided you don't give up along the way. Many people failed because they couldn't see that success was just a stone's throw away. All it would have taken was one more step, or what is called 'the extra mile'.

Most rich men and women could have admitted in retrospect that if they had thrown in the towel when the temptation was the greatest they would have missed out on success.

In the inspiring book *The Greatest Salesman in the World,* there is a passage that clearly illustrates the virtue of persistence, and the fact that it doesn't pay to be too impatient since success often likes to keep people waiting. But victory always comes to those who refuse to give up:

> Life's rewards appear at the end and not the beginning of the journey; there's no way I can foresee how many steps it will take me to reach my goal. I will perhaps meet failure at the thousandth step, and yet success will be there, hidden behind the last bend in the road. I will never know just how close I am to it if I don't [turn the corner]. I will always take one more step. If this doesn't work, I will take another, and then another... one step at a time is not so very difficult. I will persevere till I succeed.

Remember this: 'The longest journey begins with the first step. Success is sometimes found on the thousandth step and you are perhaps just a few feet away. Don't make the mistake of stopping at the 999th step, the one before success.

SUCCESS OFTEN FOLLOWS A
SERIES OF FAILURES

The lives of the rich show for the most part that they met up with numerous, sometimes spectacular, failures along the way. The same goes for many artists who became famous after having struggled for years. This is what happened to Picasso. Some time before being introduced to the public by Gertrude Stein, he went through such a bleak period that he threw out some of his paintings. He couldn't get any dealer to take them. But if Picasso had given up just before meeting Stein and had decided to pursue another career, he would never have experienced the fame he did and would never have become the multimillionaire he was. This poor, unknown artist became the richest artist in history.

On his death, his fortune was worth an estimated £500 million. But a more detailed study came to a rather different conclusion: Picasso was worth over one billion pounds.

And since three-fifths of his fortune included his personal art collection, made up of his own work and those of other masters, this figure continues to grow. These paintings' were valued at between £50,000 and £150,000, and that is without considering masterpieces such as the *Nude Woman*, painted in 1910, which was not long ago sold for over one million pounds. Picasso had almost inexhaustible energy, and sometimes finished three paintings a day. Persistence paid off for him in the end. It was the same for many other artists and actors. Most great film stars began as obscure unknowns forced to take on the most menial jobs or to accept roles in third-rate films.

There is something mysterious about success, or so it seems at first. It comes quickly and often completely unexpectedly. Many people have said that they were taken by surprise, especially since they had just recovered from a defeat. Yet, if you take a closer look, their success, albeit unexpected, was not unforeseeable. It was inevitable. Their efforts, their dreams, their investments of time, energy and courage were the seeds that they sowed.

Failures and obstacles build character. In this sense, they are profitable. The stronger your character is, the more you will be able to shape your own destiny. People who allow an initial setback to defeat them are not worthy of success. Their weak characters will make them fail. Obstacles are inevitable in any undertaking and success is rarely, if ever, achieved without having to overcome some difficulties. This is precisely what makes life a challenge.

THE RIGHT KIND OF PRIDE

People often give up because they are too proud to tolerate failure. This is the wrong kind of pride to have. This is really cowardice, and lack of self-confidence. Genuine pride is a quality shown by all these wealthy men mentioned in this book. It is the ability to persevere despite failure. Men and women who are already rich or destined to be so never doubt that success will be theirs in the end. They know that it is only a matter of time before they reap the benefits of their efforts. They know that time is inevitably on their side.

People who have the mentality of the rich never accept 'no' for a final answer. They know the value of patience. They understand that persistence and determination influence people. These qualities leave a deep impression on others. Someone working for Andrew Carnegie recounts that when he asked for his first promotion, Carnegie answered:

If you want what you are asking for with all of your heart, there is nothing I can do to prevent you from getting it.

People who want someone with all of their hearts never accept 'no' for an answer because by doing so they would be wrecking their dreams. And that, they can never accept.

Never accept 'no' for an answer

THE PSYCHOLOGY OF SUCCESS

SUCCESS IS A TEAM EFFORT

No man is an island. This saying is particularly true in business. No one can hope to get rich without the help of people around him. In other words, success is always a team effort. Sadly enough, most people seem to forget this and they neglect to cultivate their professional contacts. They isolate themselves and spend too little time developing friendships. Most of the wealthy men we analysed spoke of the vital role their partners and associates played in their success. Honda, openly confessed that had he not met a brilliant manager he would have faced bankruptcy. Onassis, was assisted by a highly talented financial administrator.

> The ability to handle people is a commodity that can be bought like sugar and coffee, and I'm willing to pay more for it than for any other.

This was what Rockefeller, who was skilful in surrounding himself with key people, declared. Think about the last part of this statement: 'I'm willing to pay more for it than for any other.' In fact, the further you advance along the road to success, the more you will notice that what counts is not so much cash, ideas, or enthusiasm, but *people*. Contacts, money, ideas, and enthusiasm, although they are important and necessary, are not enough if you can't count on people.

Learn to like people. Those who can't get along with people and who are persuaded that everybody else is always wrong will never succeed. They forget that everybody prefers working with likeable people. This may seem a platitude, but most people ignore this principle every day. They also forget that they are not the only ones who count in the world and that they are not the only ones with needs and priorities. Those who take this law into account, who are not blinded by their own egos can go far. They can have a considerable; impact on the people around them and they can work together towards success.

Success depends much more on this psychological quality than on intelligence or pure expertise. Lee Iacocca had this to say:

> Look at my own career. I've seen a lot of guys who are smarter than I am and a lot who know more about cars. And yet I've lost them in the smoke. Why? Because I'm tough? No. You don't succeed for very long by kicking people around. You've got to know how to talk to them, plain and simple. Now, there's one phrase that I hate to see on any executive's evaluation, no matter how talented he may be, and that's the line: 'He has trouble getting along with other people.' To me, that's the kiss of death. 'You've just destroyed the guy', I always think. 'He can't get along with people? Then he's got a real problem, because that's all we've got around here. No dogs, no apes — only people. And if he can't get along with his peers, what good is he to the company? As an executive, his whole function is to motivate other people. If he can't do that, he is in the wrong place.

TIPS FOR SUCCESS

Like most wealthy men, you must make friends in business. They will become your allies and will help you climb the ladder of success more quickly than you can imagine. However, be discerning in your choice of friends, especially those connected to your business. Avoid the losers, the manipulators, and those who think small. Let's examine each of these categories.

LOSERS

Start off by identifying these people. The signs of their failure are generally quite obvious. The further you proceed on the road to success, the better your ability to judge people will become. Furthermore, as your mental programming becomes more and more positive, you will begin attracting more and more winners. Above all, don't choose losers as partners, since a winner-loser combination rarely comes up with positive results no matter how strong the winner is.

The loser will cause you an enormous waste of time, energy, and money. Lastly, to reach for the top, the winner will invariably have to take over from the loser in order to re-do almost all his work from scratch. This partnership will always pull in opposite directions and is destined to fail in the long run.

All in all, the winner, despite his good intentions, will have harmed the loser, who won't feel that bad because he is used to failing. It's what he feeds on. But the pill will be harder to swallow for the winner. He will nevertheless have learned a lesson: it will reinforce his judgement in the choice of his future associates and he will never repeat the same mistake again. In any event, these two types will never get along, as they simply do not share the same fundamental values.

SCHEMERS

Their careers may appear successful at first, but are bound to fail in the long run. Those who constantly resort to shady deals and manoeuvres always end up having to account for themselves. The truth always comes out in the end. Their list of enemies keeps on getting longer and longer. Watch out for those who continually backstab associates or employees in their absence. They most likely do the same when you're not around. And anyone capable of playing dirty tricks on others can do the same to you.

SHORT-SIGHTED PEOPLE

Avoid these people like the plague. They will always stifle you because they themselves are limited. They are so narrow-minded that they cannot possibly conceive that others can enjoy a much larger vision of the world than they do. They diminish everything they come into contact with. The only thing they are good at is sapping your enthusiasm and trying to dissuade you from going ahead and embarking on new ventures. They will laugh at you if you aim high. They will label you a madman or a dreamer. Play deaf to them. Go your own way. And above all, avoid any partnership with them. You will waste your energy trying to fire them up and in convincing them to follow you. This is energy you might have used towards your own goals.

By joining forces with a winner, your chances of success will grow. In fact, the success achieved by a two-winner combination will surpass that which each of you could achieve individually. So, if you want to go far, get involved with those who are as far-sighted as you are. There will be unexpected bonuses in this alliance.

Great lessons can be learned and ideas discovered from the head-on collision of the ideas, backgrounds, and personalities of two success-orientated individuals working together. Corporate boards of directors are in fact this kind of group, each member contributing his experience and expertise. Chambers of commerce and sales associations operate in the same way. Uniting people fuelled by the same goal and values is a winning formula. However, avoid large groups. The French philosopher Montaigne put it this way: 'When men are assembled, their heads shrink."

It is not necessary to be the chairman of a company or a member of an association to take advantage of this principle. Build your own group. Choose people you trust, preferably your friends, but especially people with a positive mental attitude. This is a must. Defeatists can do immeasurable harm to an entire group. For, even in positive people, there is a shadowy area of doubt which can be affected negatively by objections and pessimistic views.

Why not set up a group with three or four members? One that will become your 'collective brain power?' They must have a common goal — that of making a fortune.

Get together on a regular basis, preferably at pre-set times. Put specific items on the agenda. The first item should be: how can we find a way to get rich? Don't stifle your ideas. Let your imagination run riot. You will probably be astonished by the number of ideas generated in this meeting. After this brainstorming session, refine your ideas. Try to analyse all the implications, applications, and concrete possibilities. One person's vague idea can be refined by someone else's suggestion and become a brilliant idea. Lay out your plans. Constructive criticism and suggestions from others will help you weigh the pros and cons.

These meetings must not be exclusively dedicated to searching for ideas. Take advantage of them to discuss the problems you have encountered at work. Exchange your ideas on your recipe for success. Discuss a book you might have read that week. Talk about strategy.

If people took the time to look carefully at the way they generally spend their evenings, they would probably be aghast at how unproductive they really are. If you want to succeed, you must dare to be different. At least once a week, or a month, have a productive, stimulating evening with your group. The results will amaze you. Let others watch TV, you cannot afford to watch TV. Nor have you the time. You are busy getting rich. Instead of wasting three hours a day in front of the television, spend only two and use the hour you saved to put you on the road to success.

LEARN TO COMMUNICATE

We are living in the midst of an information revolution. People who want to succeed must learn to express themselves clearly, firmly, and convincingly. On the road to success you are constantly called upon to persuade and convince people. So, take a public speaking course. Onassis, who spoke four languages, took one. Paul Getty learned to speak Arabic in one month by listening to recorded lessons. Try skipping TV one night and register for a language course. Speaking a second or even third language is an invaluable asset. It will also broaden your circle of contacts.

Take public speaking courses even if you show talent in this area already. Those able to talk in public are admired. What people fail to realize is that anyone can do it by taking lessons and with a little practice. The ability to speak in public, whether to a large audience or to a board meeting, will build your self-confidence, giving you a considerable advantage.

MAKE A GOOD INVESTMENT

Take a course on the art of selling. To succeed you need to be able to sell — an idea, a service, your expertise. Ultimately, you need to be able to sell yourself. Studies have shown that an individual's success is largely based on personality.

You will be called upon to do some selling no matter which field of activity you are involved in. Lawyers pleading their cases are selling themselves to the judge. Politicians making speeches are selling their government's policies. Administrators defending their budgets are selling them. Then there are those involved directly in sales. In every sphere, being familiar with sales techniques will enhance your performance.

LEARN HOW TO LISTEN

Speaking well is essential in sales. But you must also know how to listen. As a rule, people talk too much and don't listen enough. In almost every business deal, the one who knows how to listen and speaks the least is the one who gets the most out of it. The more the person you are dealing with talks, the more he opens up, revealing his motivations, needs and personality, thus allowing you to spot his weak points, which will inevitably increase your powers of influence over him. By listening attentively to people, you are showing that they interest you and are important in your eyes.

Most people love to talk. Their favourite topic is themselves. Learn to ask the right questions, so that you can show just how interested you really are in them. Observe yourself in action. What is your speaking-listening ratio? If you talk more than you listen, be careful. The other person is probably chalking up more points than you simply because he is learning more about you than you about him. Try to correct this tendency. It's merely a new habit to acquire. Try it out once. Say only the basics. Then listen. People will be delighted to have talked with you and will consider you a fine conversationalist, even though you haven't really said much.

DRESS CAREFULLY

Our world is very image-conscious. Some may think this is a shame, of course, but the fact remains the same. In all human contact, first impressions play an important role. What is the determining factor in first impressions? Usually, external things, such as a well-cut suit or dress, a warm smile, or a neat haircut. People usually judge others on their appearance. Someone sloppy generally makes a bad impression.

If you wish to succeed, dress like someone successful. If you don't know how, look around you. Get advice. Remember, all human contact contains some element of seduction. Neat, appropriate clothes go hand in hand with this. Clothes do not make the man, so the saying goes. But in business, they help a lot. Can you afford to neglect your own?

A HEALTHY MIND AND A HEALTHY BODY

This is one of the oldest maxims in the world. It is still true today. On the road to success, it is vital to stay in good shape. 'When the body is weak, it takes over command. When strong, it obeys,' said the French philosopher Jean-Jacques Rousseau. A healthy body will be your best tool in reaching for success. You will be more energetic — not only physically, but mentally as well.

Exercise regularly. It relaxes your body as much as your mind. Choose a sport that totally absorbs you and allows you to forget your professional worries.

Most of the rich men we studied took some sort of physical exercise that helped chase away the formidable tensions facing them every day. Onassis recommended judo and yoga. In fact, the first advice he gave in his recipe for success was to stay fit and healthy. He himself often went for long swims. So did Paul Getty. At the beginning of his career, Walt Disney was so overworked and neglectful of his body that he had a nervous breakdown. As soon as he was well again, he adopted a programme of relaxation and exercise.

Most great men have added physical activities to their daily routine. The great German writer Goethe went for long walks to stimulate his genius. Nietzsche claimed that ideas came to him while he was walking and thinking about things other than philosophical questions. Pope John Paul II had a swimming pool built near his living quarters. In response to one of the Vatican administrators disgruntled about this expense, he said that it would be much less expensive than setting up elections for a new pope. Pope John Paul II also goes skiing and often jogs in the Vatican gardens. That is surely one of the keys to his phenomenal physical endurance.

Follow their example and do some exercise on a regular basis.

OTHER PEOPLE'S MONEY

We have already mentioned that success is a team effort. Besides this, it is never achieved with one person's money alone. It is often the product of OPM (Other People's Money). Onassis used OPM to finance his shipping activities. He believed that behind each millionaire lies a borrower. He knew what he was talking about. Conrad Hilton also went into debt quite heavily.

Taking out loans is a delicate matter, however. For some, large loans can be catastrophic. Fluctuating interest rates can often make nasty surprises. On the other hand, without loans, many companies would never have been able to expand. Take Chrysler, for instance. It was saved by a massive loan negotiated by Lee Iacocca. Furthermore, Honda would never have been able to expand without the support of his bankers. On a more modest scale, many small investors have made handsome profits by investing $ 10,000 to buy a $ 100,000 building, resold a year later for $110,000, and so doubled their investment within a year. However, some wealthy men have shown that they did not take out loans at the beginning of their careers. They started off small and grew slowly. Then, they borrowed money.

A lesson can be learned here. It is preferable not to rely on large loans at first. It's best to start out without a luxurious office. Successful people are cost-conscious. Offices are always too large. Bankers and creditors do not want to finance luxury items.

Should you or shouldn't you borrow money? How much? When? This question is not easy to resolve. One thing is sure, though: if your subconscious is well programmed, you will know whether or not you should use OPM. Caution is always recommended. Some people never dare to borrow money and spend their lives saving up their pennies and tightening their belts, thus missing out on countless opportunities. All rich men have taken out loans at one point or other in their lives. Do as they have. But first analyse your ability to pay it back, and then rely on your instinct and subconscious mind. And don't forget that fortune favours the bold.

YOU HAVE AN INFERIORITY COMPLEX

One out of two people is reputed to suffer from low self-esteem at some point in their lives. If this is the case for you — so much the better! Think of Steven Spielberg and Soichiro Honda. Both suffered from deep inferiority complexes in their youth. But they knew how to turn it to their advantage. They didn't spend their lives bogged down in self-pity. They managed to capitalize on their complexes. You, too, can do the same. Instead of brooding over your shortcomings, you should tell yourself that you are going to become the best there is in your field.

Discover the virtues of creative frustration. The dissatisfaction you feel, no matter where it springs from, can help you go far. In one way, you will have an advantage over those with strong egos. They don't feel the need to better themselves or to change. Convert your frustration and inferiority complex into success. People will admire you.

And, as a result, you will lose your low self-esteem.

GIVE BACK PART OF WHAT YOU REAP

CHOOSE A ROLE MODEL

All those admired by someone started out admiring someone themselves. Spielberg venerated Walt Disney. Honda held Napoleon in great esteem.

Just like the great and the rich, choose an idol who will inspire you to achieve great heights. All great men had lofty ideals. They aimed high. You, too, are now aiming high. You now belong to this family of achievers. A good example is the best sermon, so the proverb goes.

A ROLE MODEL IS AN EXAMPLE TO FOLLOW

A role model can also help you in another way. When faced with a problem, ask yourself what your hero would do. You can select any wealthy person in this world.

Read the biographies of great men. Try to discover what led to their success. Use their example for inspiration. Remember that all those admired by someone started out admiring someone themselves. In the beginning, most of these men were just like you. But they applied rules that most people ignore or fail to use. You now know these principles — it's up to you to apply them and to become someone admired by all!

SELECTED BIBLIOGRAPHY

Bailey, Adrian. *Walt Disney's World of Fantasy* (Chart-well Books, 1982).

Bolton, Whitney. *The Silver Spade* (Farrar Strauss and Young, 1954).

Crawley, Tony. *The Steven Spielberg Story* (Quill Books, 1983).

Ford, Henry. My Life and Work (Doubleday, 1926).

Gawain, Shakti. *Creative Visualization* (Bantam, 1982).

Gunther, Max. *The Very, Very Rich and How They Got That Way* (Playboy Press, 1972).

Iacocca, Lee. *Iacocca* (Bantam Books, 1984).
Kroc, Ray and Anderson, Robert. *Grinding It Out: The Making of McDonald's* (Henry Regnery, 1977).

Lundberg, Ferdinand. *The Rich and the Super-Rich, A Study in the Power of Money Today* (Lyle Stuart, 1968).

McCormack, MarK *What They Don't Teach You at Harvard Business School* (Bantam Books, 1984).

Naisbitt, John. *Megatrends* (Warner Books, 1982).

Peters, Thomas J. and Waterman, Robert. *In Search of Excellence* (Warner Books, 1982).

Schreiber, David J. *Live and Be Free through Psycho-Cybernetics* (Warner Books, 1976).

Sobel, Robert. IBM: *Colossus in Transition* (Bantam Books, 1981).